How Anyone Can Invest in Crypto-Currency

(The Non-Techie Guide to Investing Successfully in Bitcoin and other Crypto-Coins)
Second Edition

By D.M. Brooks

Preface

My interest in Bitcoin began roughly five years ago when the name first started to be picked up by the news. Way back then, Bitcoin was used solely on the dark web, a place where nefarious characters at best and utter criminals at worst hung out and exchanged illegal black market items.

Bitcoin was the method of payment (still is) due to its decentralized nature and ability to use anonymously. At this time, the value of Bitcoin was about $1.00 and I was unsure of putting any money in. I also wasn't sure how to put any money in to invest.

There wasn't a simple solution that resided on the public Internet and there weren't large communities of people interested in the alt coin movement like there are today.

Looking back at this time, I wish I had a guide like this one to help explain the basics as well as show me where to go to place orders and get into the crypto-currency market.

If I had just put a sum as little as $100 into Bitcoin back then, my investment would be worth $250,000 today!

The years passed by, we saw the return of the stock market and I focused my investing in more traditional stocks and funds. It wasn't until recently when I was seeing the smoke in the news headlines that I decided to get caught up on the situation and begin making my own investments, which have turned out well to date.

My purpose for writing this book is to help you go from someone that may not know what crypto-currency even is, to someone who can take a casual interest in it and make some purchases with the hopes of future returns.

My belief is that we are entering the cusp of a radical jump in valuation for Bitcoin and alt coins in general and that during the next economic downturn, the popularity of these digital assets should increase as people look to safeguard their earnings in something not tied to centralized currency markets.

Since writing the first edition of this book, several changes have occurred both within the crypto market as well as externally that I'll be covering as we go forward.

As I write this, we've gone through a period of extreme growth followed by several corrections and bear runs.

It's important in moments like these to always remember the long-term trends and not fear the unknown.

You'll learn later how to do this and also how to protect your investments a little more when these corrections occur.

Thank you for your purchase; let's get to it.

-D.M. Brooks, October 2017.

Chapter 1: Crypto Background

Welcome to crypto-currency! Congratulations for taking the first step to being an early adopter in the next large technological revolution. You deserve credit for coming here before everyone else and I want to help you get started.

This is the second edition of my book that I decided to write after seeing so many headlines and articles written in the news about the performance of the two largest crypto-coins, Bitcoin and Ethereum (at the time of this writing). What a lot of people right now are struggling to understand is what these coins are, what they can be used for and where this whole crypto-currency thing could be going.

While I don't profess to be clairvoyant and

able to predict the future, I can write based on the past as well as give you an idea about what these coins are doing and why you should remain interested in them.

The explosion of crypto-currency over the last two years from a small online community into an attention-getting headline investment being espoused by A-list celebrities has been quite a transformation.

The growth of the last two years has been parabolic (imagine a U-curve with us in the second half) and this is only expected to continue as more people discover this investment and choose to put their money into it.

If at any time you run into something requiring additional explanation, feel free to write me your questions on Twitter @DM_BrooksCrypto and I'll respond back as quickly as I can.

In the meantime, let's dig in a little bit into what crypto-currency is, how it came about and more dealing with it's background.

To understand crypto-currency, one must first understand the limitations of fiat, or paper money and the centralization of it to governments and governing bodies (For example, the European Union).

Once paper money was disconnected from gold and silver, it turned into a system of money that had value based on perception more than any concrete physical items.

This is what we refer to when we say fiat currency; not the Italian car company.

Fiat currency is in use around the modern world, and it is a system that has the ability to increase or decrease circulation of money to help control inflation or deflation. By being controlled in a centralized fashion, governments can effectively control the wealth and the purchasing power of their citizens through the amount of money supply printed by their treasury. This has had mostly good effects if you were to look at the growth of stock markets and GDP (Gross Domestic Product) over the last fifty years. Since moving off of the Gold Standard (when all U.S. money was backed by its equivalent in physical gold) on August 15th, 1971 (when President Nixon announced the move to fiat currency), the U.S. market in particular rocketed from a DOW Jones of 856 up to it's current 22,359 of September 21, 2017. That kind of growth looks and feels great, but it can also have bad effects if there is too much paper money being printed by the treasury.

For example, the results are downright disastrous if your government isn't very stable such as what occurred in Zimbabwe during the 2000's, when the government printed currency into the trillions on paper money. By increasing the amount of paper money in circulation, it increased inflation rates a staggering 79,600,000,000% by 2008! This made the paper currency worthless for Zimbabwean citizens. Imagine being paid your current salary but not being able to afford a loaf of bread. (See image 1 below for an example of hyperinflation)

Side note: my friend Jeff snagged a couple hundred trillion in Zimbabwean money off eBay for $5 a few years back (As image 1 below shows). I'm sure that'll be worth something someday, Jeff.

(Image 1 - Or 5 times the US national debt – Sept. 2017)

That leaves us within the realm of healthy skepticism and lingering doubts about the long-term health of global economic systems at the nation-state level as long as governments continue to print money with no tangible element backing their value, however by no means is this an alarmist call to flock to digital currency. It's just to raise awareness on how much speculation, perception and belief is built into the fiat system rather than items of supreme value.

Look at the money in your bank account. Who or what ascribes value to it vs. material goods? This belief and perception in fiat money is where digital currencies are heading.

The centralization of currency, while working to most people's benefit on a macro-scale, also leads to an infinite money supply. Outside of sound fiscal and monetary policies and regulations set by legitimate governments, the fiat money supply would only be limited by the amount of currency that a government or body could print!

Trivia Time: I wonder how many printers Zimbabwe had in order to make their currency effectively worthless. This is trivia for another day.

This system of centralized currency with its lack of visibility, the perception of fiat value, as well as skepticism that bankers have society's best interests in mind (stemming from the global economic collapse of 2008-2009) are what provided the background and environment needed for the creation of crypto-currency.

Let's also not forget that there was an underground group of coding pirates that also shared these views during the global collapse, with a strong sense of libertarianism thrown into the mix.

How bad was the global collapse? While books have been written about it, let's take a look at the environment it created.

This environment where the long held belief in the stock market, Wall Street and global monetary policy came crashing down had a real impact on millions of people. For the first time in post-WW2 America, the economy stopped working for the middle class. Jobs and homes were lost in this economic churn. This economic attack on the American Dream led the charge for a consortium of computer code ninjas to start work on a new system of currency. One that would be decentralized with no central power dictating currency flow, built on a public ledger and able to sent peer to peer. This idea of decentralization, where there would be no middlemen or banks taking fees out of other people's money, is a revolution we have not seen in currency successfully before. This is a libertarian idea of deregulated currency with no government oversight. That 2008 flash point in economic history was the impetus for Bitcoin and the crypto-currency revolution. An ideology only goes so far, so what about the profits? Well, to date, Bitcoin and other coins have created a new class of billionaires and millionaires unlike most stock investments of the last decade. This new class of wealthy investors can be as young as 14 years old since the only limiting factor was access to computer networks and a Google search. This shift in wealth generation away from traditional stocks and into crypto-currencies is crucial to showcasing the potential and promise of the crypto-currency movement.

While the crypto-currency movement has grown by staggering amounts the last few years, as with most large increases in market value, there are pessimists ready to decry the movement as a bubble.

If you are an alarmist or contrarian, this may

be the wrong book for you. If you truly believe that we are witnessing a technological revolution within currency, or at least the earliest stages of a new payment method then hold on because we are going to enjoy this together as the early-adopters to a transformative technology.

As a general rule in investing, it's important to note that past performance does not guarantee future performance so if at any point you are feeling uneasy or ready to pull out of the crypto-market, that is entirely your decision and at your own discretion.

While I wouldn't put all of my children's college savings into crypto-currency, I do feel relatively confident that the value will increase over time and that we are not in a bubble (image 2 below).

That is up to you to decide, but I wouldn't have written an entire book on a passing trend. Keep in mind that the same people advising against these coins back in 2011 are still there now doing the same fear mongering that costs people money in lost opportunity.

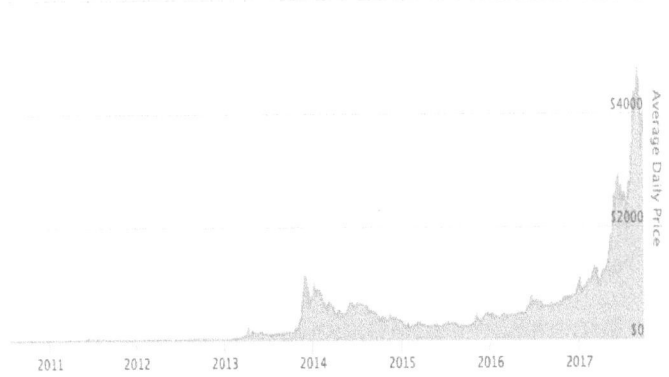

(Image 2- If you invested in Bitcoin back in 2011, you aren't reading this book)

Skepticism towards new technology is both expected and healthy; however playing it safe offers the lowest returns in investments.

While you never want to put everything you own into one basket, there's little harm in betting in crypto-currency as long as it is with money that you can afford to lose. That doesn't mean that you will automatically lose money, just be prepared and know that as with all investments, there is risk.

Another way to think about crypto-currency is as the natural progression of technology. Way back in the beginning in time, products were bartered with rocks, stones, rare minerals, materials, gold and silver.

As the world grew and countries were formed, wars started to be fought over these natural resources since they could not be duplicated.

The ability to carry these minerals was also limited, which made transactions pretty difficult to accomplish too. (Imagine buying a home in rocks). Once the printing press was invented, countries began to print their own specific money that could be used within their borders. The advent of paper money was incredible! Amounts of gold, silver and other trinkets of value could be linked to a simple piece of paper that could be easily transported.

This system of paper lasted for centuries and it was not until the age of the Internet where the next major shift began in money: the use of data to transfer money online.

Much like how the Internet turned brick and mortar stores into eBay shops, crypto-currency aims to turn the piece of paper in your wallet or bank into a digital coin, which can be used for all transactions using the Internet.

This evolution from newspapers and magazines to websites is reflected once again by turning cash and physical mineral assets into digital value stores (or coins).

When we refer to crypto-currency think of it as a new world of technology just starting to form itself. The next chapter will explain this further.

Chapter 2: What is Crypto-Currency?

Crypto-Currency is a digital asset that can be used for transactions, and acts just like traditional currency except it is entirely digital and online. There are no actual coins or paper money associated with crypto-currency. It's essentially 1's and 0's in thin air, delivered through computer networks and showing up in your trading or bank account. Imagine ordering this book off of Amazon and instead of using your credit card or PayPal, you just send me coins digitally.

Rather than using your credit card number, you would put in the amount you wish to send and then type in the unique address of the person that is receiving the payment, by clicking send the transaction is then on its way.

Same concept and method to use Amazon, only the payment source and routing has changed. Crypto-currency acts like any other kind of currency but with several key differences, advantages and disadvantages, which I will outline below:

The very first difference is that crypto-currency is not centralized. No government, no controlling entity, no sanctioning body, no company, nor any one person controls it. In order to make system or network changes, Bitcoin developers and miners need to come to an agreement.

This is what happened with the hard fork that occurred in August 2017 when Bitcoin Cash was created from a split in this community.

Crypto-currency can also be limited in production.

For example, Bitcoin (the most popular of all crypto-coins based on market cap as of this writing) is limited to 21 million coins. Litecoin, another crypto-coin, is limited to 84 million coins. Meanwhile, Ethereum (yet another coin—just wait) has no limits to its amount of coins currently. This has a slight impact on coin value in theory. Powerful computer farms, instead of using printers to print more paper money, can mine crypto-currency.

What is mining?

Mining is when these banks of computers on shelf racks are crunching the advanced calculations required to develop crypto-coins.

Some coins require more processing power than others but its safe to say that the computers required are beyond consumer grade laptops or desktops. (You can learn more about mining, cloud mining and other methods in chapter 8).

The average consumer mining setup starts around $300 and can go up from there. While it's nice to dream of building a mining rig to make money in the background while you go about your daily routine, it's important to know that due to electricity costs in the U.S., mining is very difficult to do profitably.

Because of the electrical costs, very few of us will make money mining ourselves. It costs money to make less money!

Coins created are essentially digital signatures that have been completed through advanced mathematical calculations done by these racks of powerful computers. With a coin created, the next thing you're going to want to do is to use it for a transaction. How are transactions different with crypto-coins? Well, first transactions are publicly recorded in the blockchain. This statement carries a lot of information that I will break down and simplify for you. Blockchain is the underlying technology behind the entire crypto-currency technology. To quote and paraphrase Wikipedia, "Blockchain is a distributed database that is used to maintain a continuously growing list of records, called blocks. Each block contains a timestamp and a link to a previous block. A blockchain is resistant to modification of data by design, once a block is recorded, it cannot be altered retroactively without the alteration of all subsequent blocks and a collusion of the network majority." What does this mean for crypto-currency? Simply that the ledger for all transactions conducted is public, recorded, able to be verified, won't allow for double payments, and is essentially permanent in recording these transactions which prevents fraudulent changes to transactions later (cooking the books).

Blockchain is extremely important because it facilitates the ability for a decentralized currency. With no centralized overhead controlling ledgers, the blockchain can operate openly and without potential for fraudulent bookkeeping.

The amount of technology in the blockchain and crypto-currency in general is rapidly advancing and changing seemingly every month.

It is important for you to stay informed of these changes by visiting crypto-news sites, twitter accounts, and Reddit in order to stay informed. Since all of crypto-currency is based on digital assets tied to blockchain technology, you will need to gain a sense of digital knowledge about them and their specific functions and features. That's not to say that you will need to know every byte that goes into each coin, but some idea of the roadmap for each coin is a better way to figure out the potential market value of your investment. It will also guide you with selecting which feature set is more likely to be successful over another.

Another point to bring up is that while these technologies are improving and expanding through adoption, what becomes mainstream later may not look anything like what we are seeing right now.

Take Ethereum for example:

This is a powerful blockchain technology, not truly a currency, that may result in great changes in financial banking or it could help power AI in the future. It's still very early, so the investment bet with Ethereum is on potential and promise of the blockchain application technology more than it being a currency.

We've learned several key items about what crypto-currency consists of in this section, but this has been a high level overview. If you would like to learn more, I highly suggest reading crypto-specific news sites and blogs. I'll mention a few in the additional resources section at the end of this book to get you started.

When doing your research, it's important to make sure that you are getting information from a reputable source that is not tied directly to anyone that is invest in a particular coin. Lately, there has been a lot of focus on fraudulent coins that are developed for elaborate pump and dump schemes.

The goal is generate enough interest in a crypto-coin through the use of white papers and marketing.

After the interest is achieved, an ICO date (or initial coin offering) is scheduled for people to buy in, much like an IPO (initial public offering) on the stock market.

Not all coins or ICOs are equal and the SEC (Securities and Exchange Commission), as well as China are investigating and in China's case, outright banning the practice of ICOs due to the amount of scams that have occurred with fake coins.

Buyers beware when looking into alternate coins.

As you invest in coins, always ask yourself, "What problem is the coin trying to solve?" Who are the developers? Is this a pump and dump scheme ICO that is intended to only make the founders rich? How many people are investing in it? What is the market cap?

ICOs and smaller coins will require you to do your research. Much like the Internet of the 1990's, some companies (or coins) will be scams and some will be the next Amazon, eBay, Alibaba, etc. It is very important to recognize that since the market is still so new, there will be a bit of a Wild West factor to it.

You will only be 100% safe if you stick with the proven coins and avoid ICOs.

By sticking with the coins that have the largest market caps, you are going to be a safer investor that will not have to worry about scammers and ICOs. At least not until more controls are put in place to protect investors.

This is one of the risks of being an early adopter in any technology.
While it may not be coins, it would be something or someone else looking to take advantage of new investors to any deregulated market.

Once all transactions are recorded publically and there's no reasonable ability to go back and change an entry, it's going to be harder and harder to launder money, if not impossible.

Think of the ways this would benefit our banking systems, financial reporting, stock markets and company quarterly reports if nothing could be hidden related to transactions.

Hopefully this helps to paint a picture of what crypto-currency is and why it's received so much attention from early adopters and investors.

At the bare minimum, it promises more accuracy in recording of transactions, a huge reduction in potential fraud, the end of double counting and a system that is nearly impossible to take over and attack (thousands or millions of computers all separated track each transaction – good luck trying to hack every one of them in order to change the blockchain).

Now that you understand the technology behind crypto-currency, you may want to know how it can be used in your daily life. The answer is both simple and nuanced which we will get into in the next chapter.

Chapter 3: How Is Crypto-Currency Used?

Before I describe how it can be used, you are going to need to know the advantages, disadvantages and a basic rundown of what crypto-currency is.

What are the advantages to crypto-currency? Well, with the currency based on a blockchain, the ledger is public and highly secure due to the distributed nature of the database that it is on. This means that double transactions are no longer possible and no central authority is needed to oversee transactions since they are secured (and unable to be reasonably altered).

With the advantage of a highly secure distributed network that publically records transactions and makes double spending impossible, crypto-currency also has the advantage of not being limited by the economic conditions of the state or country that its users are in.

This means that inflation and a Zimbabwe disaster are kept in check through the inability to just print more money.
This is especially important when discussing Bitcoin or other currencies with a set maximum amount of coins. As supply of the coins runs out, the currency will actually have a deflationary effect.

The deflationary aspect of Bitcoin is when the limited number of coins available means value will continue to increase along with its purchasing power.
This is unlike the US Dollar, where printing more money only lessens the purchasing power of one dollar.

Due to the decentralized nature of crypto-currency, this also means that crypto-currency is not limited by the borders of the user's country. A buyer in Japan can transact with a seller in the UK without having to pay conversion fees or lose value since crypto isn't tied to any single county's monetary system.

Another way it can be used is as an investment, which is why you're reading this book. As an investment, it is important to realize that the largest gains with any new technology occur the earlier you invest in the market.

As Geoffrey Moore has written extensively about, there are stages to any new technology. It's important that you learn about these stages and how they will impact the upcoming revolution of crypto-currency. (See Image 3)

To highlight the main message about crypto-currency investing, we are no longer in the innovator period.

Instead we are now in early adopter mode, which is a great place to be as an investor because it's before the mainstream gets involved (institutional banks, investors with large holdings, mom and dad, etc.). Here is a visual overview of how the progression of new technology occurs:

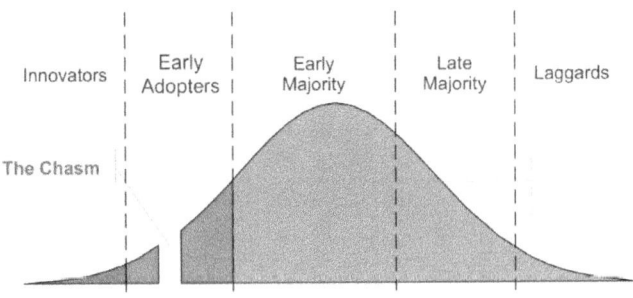

(Image 3 – The technology adoption curve)

The innovators are the people who developed and bought into Bitcoin before 2012. They are now the millionaires and billionaires helping to shape the future of crypto-currency or enjoying life on their yacht. Maybe both.

What you will find after them are the early adopters like us that see the potential for a massive wave of change. As of late 2017, we are going to be transitioning over the next year or two into the Early Majority period as large banking institutions, well-known investors and vast sums of money begins to get involved in Bitcoin. (A Bitcoin IRA is even around now!)

What all of this means is quite clear: If Jaime Dimon is right, and Bitcoin is a "fraud that will just blow up", then it's going to blow up the largest institutions with it.

(Side Note: While speaking about Bitcoin as a fraud, JP Morgan Securities was caught buying Bitcoin in large chunks on foreign exchanges. Yet another advantage of having a public ledger.)

So how can crypto-currency be used? Many different ways, much like any legal tender. However there is one more usage for it that is going to be a large advantage internationally:

It can be used as a safe harbor of stored value for when fiat based economies struggle or go into recessions.

Since crypto-currency is completely separate from fiat, it does not possess direct ties to the fortunes of the global stock markets. Instead, it will act as a place to store money while the traditional markets collapse during the cyclical recessions that occur.

A shrewd investor would simply move their assets around during this time to help protect their wealth. This would lead to even greater gains to investors of crypto-currency that had held on from before the recession took place.

Now with the basic advantages out of the way, its important to note the disadvantages of crypto-currency.

For the first disadvantage, crypto-currency is only online. There are no physical coins that have value off of the Internet at this current time. What this means is that unless the transaction is capable to be completed online where crypto-currency is accepted, you won't be able to use it without converting it back to fiat.

This accessibility to the crypto-coins in everyday life is slowly changing for the better, but it will be a few years before your local Target or Wal-Mart will accept them.

However, with that said, there are rumors that Amazon will be accepting Bitcoin soon and Overstock.com has accepted crypto-currency now for over two months! The tide is changing, and soon you will start to see the familiar Bitcoin accepted here logo at most cash registers.

Another disadvantage of crypto-currency is that we simply cannot predict accurately where their value is going to be 5-10 years from now. We can forecast and project, but no one truly knows how much a Bitcoin will be worth in 2025. If they say that they do, don't use them for investment advice. (I will provide projections later in this book, but caveat emptor).

Finally, the other main disadvantage that you need to be aware of is that cyber attacks do happen and people have lost their coins through them. As a matter of being an online citizen of the global Internet, I'm assuming that you practice a good approach to your cyber security. The very first rule of investing in crypto-currency is to not talk about investing in crypto-currency. The ultimate defense against losing your hard-earned coin stash is to buy a hardware wallet for them. I will show you how to setup a hardware wallet later in this book in Chapter 7. Out of the hardware wallets available, I can recommend the Trezor or Ledger Nano S to store your coins offline safely.

Good security practices are a must if you start to invest beyond a casual amount that you're ok with losing.

With that said, as long as you aren't leaving thousands of dollars on open exchanges, sharing the amount you have invested, publically list your email address and go on Reddit to tell people: you'll more than likely be ok.

As we discussed in the advantages section, crypto-currency (mainly Bitcoin) can be used to conduct transactions online with a few online vendors as well as make payments in Japan and elsewhere that Bitcoin is accepted. This acceptance is expected to grow internationally and signs of gradual acceptance are becoming more frequent. There are now Bitcoin ATMs popping up around the US too, for those of you so inclined. This payment is slowly spreading and within the decade, expect it to be used to order nearly everything you could possibly want online or in person.

As an investor eager to make money, you now know that crypto-currency's best use right now is as a store of value. You invest your fiat into it and wait for it to gain acceptance, go mainstream and have large investors come into the market in order to raise its value. If you are so inclined to trade with it, you can ride the waves of appreciation and depreciation to make some returns as well. Heck, you can even day trade crypto-currency just like stocks with some trading platforms that I'll mention later in Chapter 9. Several people do this and have made a lot of money just by applying some old fashioned Technical Analysis to different coins. While not as stable as the traditional American stock market, it can be vastly rewarding to those that time their trades correctly.

Hopefully, this basic rundown provides you with a backdrop of the highlights of crypto-currency. You now understand the basic theory of the blockchain, what crypto-currency can and cannot do, as well as what it's advantages and disadvantages are at this current time.

I'd only like to add one more thought before ending this chapter: Crypto-currency is a risk, but an educated risk that is based on sound computer science principals and next generation technology which has the capability of altering the way we use money across the planet. We are currently where the Internet was back in 1994, so expect major disruptive market forces to come in the future. Reading this book in 2017 gets you ahead of the learning curve for many future investors but know that there are many before now that have already made their fortunes. May we all be so lucky.

As a side note, every mainstream news source seems to all use the same tired story about how some guy ordered pizza with Bitcoin back in (insert the year) and how that pizza today would cost (insert here). The figures are sensationalist yet true. The value has only continued to increase every year once you pull back the macro lens. For this reason, among the others listed, you will make money as an early adopter if you play your coins right.

These large gains come with a cost though, and it's important that you follow the tax laws of your country. For the next section, we will cover what the IRS (Internal Revenue Service) says about crypto-currency.

Chapter 4: Taxes and Crypto

In the first edition, we never covered the tax implications of investing in crypto-currency. I had assumed that people would know that you are taxed on investment gains in the U.S. and must pay the IRS the taxes required from it. It wasn't until I was asked directly about if I paid taxes on my own gains that it came to me that people are not sure where Bitcoin or crypto-coins fit within the tax codes. As amazing as crypto-currency is, as decentralized as it may be, you have to pay taxes on it. I would never tell anyone to not pay taxes on their crypto-investments. What I can do is help guide you a little on what to do and how to prepare for taxes with your crypto-investments.

Note that I am not a CPA (Certified Public Accountant), nor am pretending to be one.

I would recommend that you hire a CPA that is familiar with the tax codes around crypto-currency if you have trouble with TurboTax. **This section is written for the U.S. only, if you live elsewhere please research your own tax laws and consult with a professional.** Ok, with that out of the way, the very first thing to know is that crypto-currencies are defined by the IRS as PROPERTY.

What this means is that you must pay taxes on capital gains or losses every time you dispose of the crypto-currency. For example, if you buy .023 of Bitcoin for $80 and then sell .006 Bitcoin for $12, you will pay the gain or loss on that $12 sale. (These figures are just an example). Or to put it simply with round numbers: You purchase 1 Bitcoin for $2900, then sell that same 1 Bitcoin a few months later for $3800, you now owe tax on the $900 profit.

Another thing to keep in mind with crypto-currency being labeled as property is that it also is included in your income for the year. For example, Kyle makes $70,000 a year gross from his job. If he buys and sells Bitcoin like the example above, then his total taxable gross income is now $70,900 for the year.

This can have major implications for your taxes if you have invested a lot of money, bought a lot of coins, then sold them and made a lot of money. This scenario could have the effect of moving you up into a higher tax bracket where your total income is taxed at a higher rate!
In using Bitcoin as the example, I am not stating that the other coins avoid taxes. Instead, I am just using the most widely used and invested crypto-currency of 2016 for the example.

When you consult with a CPA, I'd recommend using the Bitcoin name to start your discussions about crypto-currency investments to judge how in-depth their knowledge is of these investments. From there you can discuss how you own 1,000 coins in XMR, DASH, Monero, VTC, etc. (these are other crypto-coins commonly available)

What else should you know about taxes with crypto-currency investing?

Unlike with cash, when you spend crypto currency, it is really two transactions in one: disposing of the crypto-currency and then spending the cash-equivalent amount (1 Bitcoin sold off at $3800 and taxed, then spending $3800 on an item, which may be taxed).

Business transactions in crypto-currencies are subject to all the normal rules for sales tax, withholding, and information reporting, which means that just like your other business transactions you will need to keep detailed records of every transaction in crypto-currencies so that your income is accurately measured.

Now let's investigate what the IRS classifies crypto-currency as, because this is important for understanding how to arrange your investments at tax time.

First, the IRS refers to Bitcoin and crypto-currency as "Virtual Currency". This is important when reading through the tax terms used by them in allocating Bitcoin as property.

As we've discussed, for federal tax purposes, crypto-currency is treated as property. General tax principles that apply to transactions of property apply to transactions using crypto-currency.

The IRS has published guidelines in Notice 2014-21 on their website (**https://www.irs.gov/irb/2014-16_IRB#NOT-2014-21**)

Some highlights from this notice include:

- "A taxpayer who receives virtual currency as payment for goods or services must, in computing gross income, include the fair market value of the virtual currency, measured in U.S. dollars, as of the date that the virtual currency was received."
- "Virtual currency that has an equivalent value in real currency, or that acts as a substitute for real currency, is referred to as "convertible" virtual currency. Bitcoin is one example of a convertible virtual currency. Bitcoin can be digitally traded between users and can be purchased for, or exchanged into, U.S. dollars, Euros, and other real or virtual currencies."
- "Transactions using virtual currency must be reported in U.S. dollars" on the tax return.
- "Taxpayers will be required to determine the fair market value of virtual currency in U.S. dollars as of the date of payment or receipt."

- "If a virtual currency is listed on an exchange and the exchange rate is established by market supply and demand, the fair market value of the virtual currency is determined by converting the virtual currency into U.S. dollars ... at the exchange rate, in a reasonable manner that is consistently applied."

The IRS also answers a couple relevant questions in this document, so I recommend you go and read through it, as well as provide a copy of it to your CPA at tax time. Some of these questions and answers are as follows:

Q–6: Does a taxpayer have gain or loss upon an exchange of virtual currency for other property?

A–6: Yes. If the fair market value of property received in exchange for virtual currency exceeds the taxpayer's adjusted basis of the virtual currency, the taxpayer has taxable gain. The taxpayer has a loss if the fair market value of the property received is less than the adjusted basis of the virtual currency.

Q–8: Does a taxpayer who "mines" virtual currency (for example, uses computer

resources to validate Bitcoin transactions and maintain the public Bitcoin transaction ledger) realize gross income upon receipt of the virtual currency resulting from those activities?

A–8: Yes, when a taxpayer successfully "mines" virtual currency, the fair market value of the virtual currency as of the date of receipt is includible in gross income.

Q–12: Is a payment made using virtual currency subject to information reporting?

A–12: A payment made using virtual currency is subject to information reporting to the same extent as any other payment made in property. For example, a person who in the course of a trade or business makes a payment of fixed and determinable income using virtual currency with a value of $600 or more to a U.S. non-exempt recipient in a taxable year is required to report the payment to the IRS and to the payee. Examples of payments of fixed and determinable income include rent, salaries, wages, premiums, annuities, and compensation.

In summary, what all of this means is that you must know these two basic tenants of crypto-currency at tax time (courtesy of Turbo Tax):

Bitcoins held as capital assets are taxed as property

If you hold crypto-currency as a capital asset, you must treat them as property for tax purposes. General tax principles applicable to property transactions apply to crypto-currency.

If your crypto-currency is held as a capital asset, like stocks or bonds, any gain or loss from the sale or exchange of the asset is taxed as a capital gain or loss. Otherwise, you will realize ordinary gain or loss on an exchange.

Crypto-Currency miners must report receipt of the crypto- currency as income

Some people "mine" Bitcoins, Litecoins, VTC, etc. by using computer resources to validate transactions and maintain the transaction ledger.

According to the IRS, when a taxpayer successfully "mines" crypto-currency coins and has earnings from that activity whether in the form of coins or any other form, he or she must include it in his gross income after determining the fair market dollar value of the virtual currency as of the day it was received. If a miner is self-employed, his or her gross earnings minus allowable tax deductions are also subject to the self-employment tax.

Make sure that you keep records of your transactions. Coinbase among other sites can tabulate these for you so that you have a record at tax time. It is extremely important to have the records which will allow you to calculate your short term capital gains vs. your long term gains due to the difference in tax rate/penalty for each as you continue to invest. Don't make the mistake of getting slammed with short-term capital gains taxes when you buy and sell coins for profit. Make sure to always calculate in the tax penalties when you conduct transactions on the crypto-market in order to effectively shield yourself from an unexpectedly high tax bill.

This section contains the best starting information on this topic that you could have as it comes directly from the IRS and TurboTax. It is not a substitute for consulting with a reputable CPA and at no point in time should you solely use what is contained here when doing your year-end taxes unless you are a professional accountant and understand tax code laws.

For the casual investor, this sounds a lot more complicated than it really is and if you have ever invested in stocks, you will see similarities to investing in crypto-currencies. As technical and scary as taxes can be, just remember that this is what every investor has to go through and that even the best growth potential is taxed.

Before the IRS rules were published, there were people not paying taxes on these gains from crypto-currency. This is illegal and not something you should do unless you plan to escape the federal government and be on the run for the rest of your life. The IRS has been gearing up to proceed with tax evasion investigations since 2014 and are more prepared than ever to go after you and your property for failing to disclose gains made in crypto-currency. As of this writing, there have been exchanges contacted by the IRS with the intent of them providing access to user accounts to the IRS for investigative purposes of tax evasion. Make sure you pay your taxes!

Questions or comments? Please send a message to me on twitter at @DM_BrooksCrypto or contact a CPA professional that deals in crypto-currency for their expert opinion. As always, look at the IRS guidance with the link provided and look at the basics on TurboTax's website for additional details. I will not do your taxes for you, but many others will!

Now that you've paid your taxes, let's look into all the coins you can invest in to earn gains that make the taxes that the IRS wants so interesting.

Chapter 5: What Coins are Available?

A better question would be what coins are not available these days. What Bitcoin started back in 2009 has now expanded to hundreds and hundreds of coins that are across the Internet.

Due to Bitcoin's success, copycat coins and scam coins (the previously mentioned ICOs) have been created to try to artificially build a market to make a select few rich. Much like the Wild West, it's important to separate these hoax coins from the stable mainstream coins that have gained wide acceptance.

For every Bitcoin, Litecoin or Ethereum, there are coins based on Internet jokes or memes (not to pick on one, but Dogecoin is based on a meme). Since this is a decentralized space, free market rules apply here.

I would advise against taking substantial investments in coins that are scams. A good way to know if the currency is not legitimate is to monitor the coins available on the major trading platforms.

For the purposes of this book, I'll talk about a very limited set of three coins, which are available on the easiest exchange to use, Coinbase. If this strikes more curiosity into other coins or exchange platforms, then this book has been a good guide.

Before I get questions about why I left out XX coin or exchange, please understand that this isn't intended to be an all-encompassing foray into the hundreds (nearing thousand) of coins that currently exist.

Bitcoin

You can't speak about crypto-currency without hearing the name Bitcoin. So let's start there. Bitcoin is the largest and oldest crypto-currency coin, having been created back in 2009 by a completely unknown developer using a fake name. Mr. Satoshi Nakamoto was a pseudonym used by one, maybe two people (depending on which theory you'd like to subscribe to) who had a vision for a truly decentralized currency that wouldn't be controlled by the banking system that just blew up the global markets.

The disastrous fallout from that global recession only strengthened the resolve that a decentralized form of currency was necessary to protect people from something like that happening again.

Satoshi is a name of legend and lore to the crypto-community and if having a false name doesn't sound professional, think to yourself what type of attention, both positive and mostly negative, that the creator of the very first large scale decentralized currency would find them in. His invention, Bitcoin, has successfully risen from an experiment in blockchain technology to the preeminent crypto-currency that has turned normal people into multi-billionaires and millionaires seemingly overnight.

The reality is a little different than overnight, as seen below:

- January, 2009 Bitcoin introduced (price = $0)
- January 1, 2010 Bitcoin price = $0.01
- January 1, 2011 Bitcoin price = $0.30
- January 1, 2012 Bitcoin price = $5.27
- January 1, 2013 Bitcoin price = $13.30

- January 1, 2014 Bitcoin price = $770.44
- January 1, 2015 Bitcoin price = $313.92
- January 1, 2016 Bitcoin price = $434.46
- January 1, 2017 Bitcoin price = $1,005.42

As of this writing, Bitcoin has doubled since January and is currently trading above $4,300 a coin.

The benefit to being the front-runner of crypto-currency is found in the coin's value and in it's wide acceptance in the crypto-community. This has its downsides though, and I'll list them out for you here.

The first downside is that Bitcoin is limited to 21 million coins. This means that as the supply gets bought up, it will be harder and harder for most people to afford 1 coin. That makes it harder to get rich off of Bitcoin since the buy-in cost of multiple coins continues to increase.

The second downside is that since Bitcoin was the first technology released, it will also need to continue to add new functionality and features to it in order for it to maintain relevancy in a rapidly changing world of blockchain.

Lastly, the third downside is that mining (remember that?) has become economically impossible for anyone but large farming racks in China where electricity costs are dirt-cheap. Your laptop won't be able to mine coins in the background while you watch cat videos on YouTube profitably.

Now, what are the advantages?

Realistically, Bitcoin isn't going away anytime soon. It's the most valuable, most widely used, most visible and has the most acceptance across the world (For example, Japan and popular ecommerce sites have started to accept payments in Bitcoin).

Listed as a downside, but the limited supply of coins also means that as supply runs out, prices will increase with more demand, which means upside for early investors.
This makes holding onto your Bitcoin a wise method to make money off of your investment.

Bitcoin is the father of the crypto-currency movement and the most viable alternative to fiat that currently exists due to these favorable factors.

It has the most media attention, the most institutional attention and its own IRA now! While that could simply mean that it could be the next MySpace to another coin's Facebook, it does not preclude you from taking profits in it in the meantime.

Now what if we took Bitcoin's blockchain technology, added in some additional technologies for smart contracts, scaling, removed the limits on amount of coins produced and even allowed developers to build applications off of the blockchain?

Ethereum has the most potential of the three coins being discussed due to the capabilities beyond currency such as smart contracts and applications. However, it is still early in trying to decide where Ethereum's value will go as a currency. There are a lot of uses for Ethereum as a blockchain technology that have yet to expand beyond the early beginnings of a technology with major potential.

This could be a good investment if smart contracts and all the synergies come alive with Ethereum and the applications that run off of its blockchain.

Ethereum even has clone blockchains built off of its open source nature!

This just adds more potential to the investment.

See, unlike Bitcoin, Ethereum is actually a new open software platform based on blockchain technology that enables developers to build and deploy decentralized applications.

This means that if a new application is delivered that has widespread acceptance and is a game changing app, the entire platform increases in value. What is nice about Ethereum is that since it's not tied to being a singular coin, but rather a platform, you have MULTIPLE chances to make money off of it.

Now with that said, nothing has really happened with its applications just yet. There are some heavy investments being put into Ethereum technology and big name investors like Mark Cuban are getting involved with it. There will continue to be a lot of attention paid towards Ethereum due to the open source nature of its blockchain and widespread knowledge and acceptance of it. Yet unlike Bitcoin, there just hasn't been that killer singular use for it developed just yet.

The main takeaway with Ethereum is that unlike Bitcoin, it is much more than a currency.

The future for its use remains to be seen, but it is a very bright future just lacking the one or many game changing uses for it. Think 1994 Internet before AOL carried it into every home. To further that analogy, Ethereum just needs its AOL app. This is another good investment to have in your portfolio.

The last of the three major crypto-currency coins that this book will cover is Litecoin. Litecoin is an interesting case study. What if we took the Bitcoin model, expanded it's limited amount from 21 million coins to 84 million coins and added in additional technologies like segwit, lightening network capability and atomic swap capabilities (will explain this in a bit) in order to speed up transactions by several minutes over Bitcoin.

You may find people comparing Litecoin as the silver to Bitcoin's gold and while this wouldn't be far off from a technology perspective, what has yet to happen is for Litecoin to rapidly grow in value.

This lack of growth has trended more towards stability, but additional technologies and functionality over Bitcoin are being added within this past year that helped to expand its market cap and footprint.

Beyond adding in the new functionalities, Litecoin has expanded to different trading platforms and countries. This has also had a positive impact on it's price valuation in the last year. However of the three coins listed in this book, you will find Litecoin offering the most value from the perspective of having the lowest cost to buy into at the current time (roughly $53 a coin).

Many crypto-investors believe that of the major 3, Litecoin is undervalued due to its technical abilities and future roadmap under Charlie Lee.

Why invest in Litecoin if it has these abilities but without parabolic (that U-curve again) growth? For many of the same long term reasons as Bitcoin, Litecoin is a growing stable crypto-currency that provides technological advances over Bitcoin (much like other competing coins), while still providing ease of accessibility to purchasing the coin.

As expansion onto new trading platforms has occurred, there is momentum to continue growth of the coin development and a growing community around Litecoin.

When speaking about crypto-currency as an investment, Litecoin belongs in your portfolio for the following reasons:

First, it has an excellent engineering team behind it led by Charlie Lee (who goes by the name SatoshiLite on twitter – jokes, people). This team has been able to produce some of the more interesting currency developments out there this past year and with Charlie at the helm it won't slow down.

The big change to Litecoin that occurred this year was the implementation of the segregated witness technology (segwit for short).

"SegWit is the process by which the block size limit on a blockchain is increased by removing signature data from Bitcoin transactions. When certain parts of a transaction are removed, this frees up space or capacity to add more transactions to the chain.

"Segregate means to separate, and Witnesses are the transaction signatures. Hence, "Segregated Witness in short, means to separate transaction signatures." – Investopedia.

What this means is that the amount of transactions that can be handled by the blockchain is increased substantially since the blocks themselves within the blockchain are increased in size.

This increase in block size (1MB to 4MB) as well as stripping the signature data from transactions allows for each block to handle more transactions, which speeds up the blockchain process, allowing for Litecoin to have faster transactions.

The next technology introduced on Litecoin that has major potential for turning Litecoin into an everyday currency, is the addition of the Lightning Network to the coin.

What does this mean?

Instant Payments. Lightning-fast blockchain payments without worrying about block confirmation times. Security is enforced by blockchain smart-contracts without creating an on-blockchain transaction for individual payments. Payment speed measured in milliseconds to seconds.

Scalability. Capable of millions to billions of transactions per second across the network. Capacity blows away legacy payment rails by many orders of magnitude. Attaching payment per action/click is now possible without custodians.

Low Cost. By transacting and settling off-blockchain, the Lightning Network allows for exceptionally low fees, which allows for emerging use cases such as instant micropayments.

Cross Blockchains. Cross-chain atomic swaps can occur off-chain instantly with heterogeneous blockchain consensus rules. So long as the chains can support the same cryptographic hash function, it is possible to make transactions across blockchains without trust in 3rd party custodians. (www.lightning-network.com)

With the introduction of the last two technologies to Litecoin, it has turned itself as not only the silver to Bitcoin's gold, but as a real potential currency which could be used day to day for small transactions that need to happen instantly. You could buy a coffee in line with Litecoin with these two technologies enabled! That provides Litecoin with a real investment argument that the other coins mentioned do not currently have: a use case.

Lastly, with Litecoin there is now the capability to perform Atomic Swaps. Atomic Swaps are genius and here is why. Say you have 50 Bitcoins in your account and you want to buy something, but the store only accepts Litecoin.

(This isn't likely to ever be the case, but work with me here). Atomic swaps will allow you to exchange your Bitcoin for Litecoin instantly without having to go through an exchange or 3rd party (which charges you for the right to exchange your own currency). Imagine the flexibility that this will bring. No matter what the shop or need for currency type may be, you can easily, instantly perform an exchange without fees with Litecoin.

Atomic swaps also help to keep decentralization alive and well in crypto-currency since no 3rd party or exchange will be needed to convert Litecoin to another type of crypto-coin.

An example provided by The Merkle for Atomic Swaps is, "Atomic Swaps allows users to cross-trade different crypto currencies without relying on centralized parties. If user A has Bitcoin, and user B wants Ethereum Classic, for example, they can agree to a fixed trading price and complete the transaction immediately."

When talking Bitcoin, it's important to note that it is the first to market and the largest, but it is not the most technologically advanced and is a few revisions behind where Litecoin currently is positioned along the technology roadmap. This could lead to a reversal of fortunes with Bitcoin and another coin in the future, but for now it seems that there is a symbiotic relationship between Bitcoin and Litecoin values.

As Bitcoin rises, so does Litecoin as the silver to the gold. Where this ends up is projected later in this book, but the prognosis is positive overall. Meanwhile, Ethereum has multiple avenues to become a winner and it can be outside of crypto-currency altogether with its open source blockchain technology. The future is bright indeed.

In summary, these three coins all possess the long-term investment opportunity that crypto-currency has for early adopters. They each have their strengths and each have potential to do much more over the coming years.

Chapter 6: How to Setup an Account

By this point you know a decent amount about the three major coins being traded on the Coinbase platform. If you've gotten to this point, you're ready to dip your toes into the crypto-currency market and I will show you how to sign up to a Coinbase account and start your investing.

First, go to www.coinbase.com and register a new account. You will need to provide an email address, your name, physical address, and a bank account or credit card for transactions. The credit card option is quicker to make purchases with, but it has a much lower weekly dollar limit on the amount of coins you can buy.

For me personally, I prefer to use the credit card transactions since it is an almost instant purchase that shows up in your Coinbase account quickly vs. the bank account purchase option where the purchase is instant but the funds won't show up in your Coinbase account for up to 5 business days.

As people start out, they may have a lot of discretionary income to invest with and the low weekly money limit prevents them from buying as many coins as they'd like.
If this sounds family, follow the steps below and Coinbase will increase your weekly limits on both your credit card purchases as well as your bank account purchases.
 It isn't hard to do and it doesn't take long, but it will require more identity verification in order to keep transactions safe and secure on the site for everyone.

To increase your weekly buy and sell limits for your credit (or debit) card you may need to complete several of the following verification steps:

- Verify your account
    - Verify your email address
    - Verify your phone number
- Complete your personal details
    - Full name
    - Date of birth
    - Residential address
- Add payment methods
    - Add bank account details
    - Add credit card details
    - Add debit card details
- Verify your identity
    - Taxpayer identification number
    - Government-issued identification document
    - Identity verification by answering a few questions

- Complete a purchase through Coinbase

You may not have to provide all of the above verification steps, as they can be different depending on your geographic location or account features.

(Image 5- After your identity and information are entered, your weekly limits increase greatly)

After you have verified your identity and bank account information (Image 5 above) you will also have a login and password provided. Make sure you memorize, write down and secure this information safely. Coinbase is now ready for you to use.

As you use it, your weekly limits will increase along with your holdings as you buy and sell coins.

The Coinbase website uses two factor authentication to help provide an extra layer of account security. It is important to never share your login information on the Internet. Going back to the risks of crypto-currency…keep your information secure and private.

You may access Coinbase either through your computer, or through the mobile app that is available for both Android and the iPhone. I like to split my time between the two because the website offers more tools to view coin performance than the mobile app does, however the mobile app is perfect for making purchase decisions on the fly as the market changes.

With the website account setup and the mobile app on your phone, you now have access from anywhere to your account and coins. Congratulations, you're now on the cusp of investing in crypto-currency with the easiest to use platform currently available. Think of Coinbase as the PayPal for crypto-currency and the functions become similar and more familiar to use.

With the wide availability of Coinbase and the acceptance it has received on Reddit and other forum communities for simple purchases for beginners, the likelihood that Coinbase continues to grow is quite strong.

In fact, Coinbase has recently raised funds (over $1 billion USD) to expand its customer service operations as the growth of its customer base has exceeded what they could support!

This bodes very well for Coinbase being the standard for people to purchase the main three currencies in the future as well as shows stability to the market overall.

I would setup your account here until you are more comfortable with the other services offered (or make enough money to need more control on the minute by minute action). The only downside to Coinbase is that it is not a trading platform for day traders to use. This limitation is why many will only use it to purchase coins and then send them to their accounts elsewhere for trading purposes (or to buy coins not listed on Coinbase).

Some of these other platforms are Bittrex, Poloniex and GDAX. A lot of people use Polo and Bittrex these days as the accepted sites for day trading or to invest in alternative coins (dubbed "altcoins") that don't appear on Coinbase.

You will also see yet more sites that service South Korea and other non-U.S. countries. It is your choice which site fits your needs the best. Personally, I use Coinbase for the big 3 and then Bittrex and Polo both to invest in altcoins as well as to send and receive coins to my hardware wallet. As a beginner to crypto, Coinbase is still the easiest to use and send coins from.

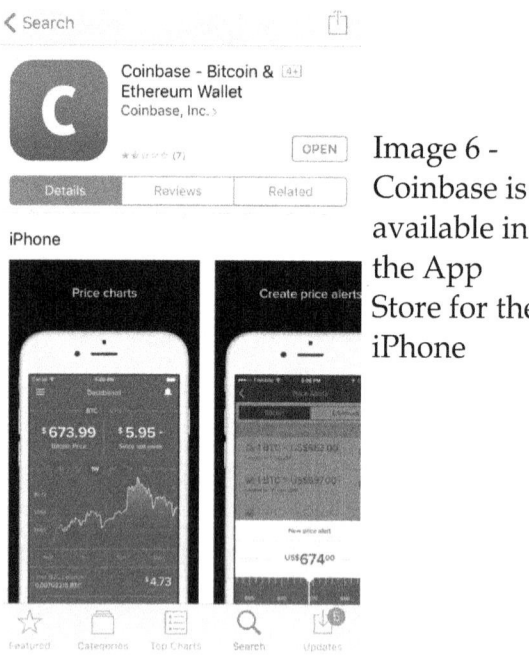

Image 6 - Coinbase is available in the App Store for the iPhone

When discussing sending money or coins across the Internet as well as putting your identity and banking information into a website it is very important that basic security guidelines and recommendations are followed. I know that I am repeating myself here, but as more hacking exploits hit the mainstream media, it should be readily apparent why I keep bringing this up.

As with all new technologies, there are risks associated with the crypto-exchanges and hacking is one of them. It is vitally important to practice good Internet sanitation and to keep your amounts private.

There have been people who have advertised their holdings and have been hacked and had them stolen. If you consider that Equifax can be hacked or many, many other major corporations with whole teams of IT security professionals inspecting data traffic experience attacks, it's best to stay private and use good security sense when investing in crypto.

Please do not make yourself a target; there are way too many bad people out there that don't need any more help.

Also, please use two-factor authentication on your account, do not share your passwords and get a hardware wallet if you plan on carrying high balances. These are some strategies to help you navigate the waters of early technology adoption and minimize the risks. The ability to buy and sell coins on Coinbase with some good Internet security will allow you to enjoy this investment for years to come.

You now have the information you need to invest in the main 3 coins listed on Coinbase. You also know that if it's a lot of money for you, do not leave it on Coinbase, but transfer it to a cold wallet (offline hardware storage). We will go into how to do that later in this book in Chapter 7.

This is all a repeat of what's been said earlier, but I am writing it because of how important this is to protect you and your investments.

Do not leave your coins on an exchange.
Make sure you transfer them to a hardware
wallet.

If you want to see the worst-case scenario,
look into Mt. Gox. Users of Mt. Gox lost an
estimated $400 million dollars from theft
because too many people left their coins on
the exchange.

Imagine waking up one morning, thinking
you're a millionaire and logging in to check
your account balance in Bitcoins, only to find
out that it's all gone without a trace.

Don't be a victim. We want you to have a
yacht (or at least a realistic looking model of
one) and help humanity after all.

So with the security talk out of the way, how can you protect your investment from online thieves? By using a hardware wallet to store your coins.

This leads us to the next Chapter nicely.

Chapter 7: How to Setup a Hardware Wallet:

This is your best friend for safe storage of your coins.

As mentioned, the risks of keeping your coins on an exchange are high enough to not do it long-term.

When you need to hold onto your coins, there are two options: a "hot" wallet or a "cold" wallet.
A hot wallet is one that is online. Coinbase now offers a hot wallet through the use of its Vault technology that is offered through its website.

There are quite a few other online wallets that are available too, but for the purposes of this book and security in general – store your coins offline.

Anything connected to the Internet has a real possibility of being hacked and stolen. I don't care what levels of security are promised, all it takes is one patch to be missed and a knowledgeable hacker could compromise the entire system. With the amount of money involved in crypto-currency, along with the inability to truly track it down, there are a lot of incentives for hackers to get into these online storage vaults.

This leaves us with option B: the cold wallet. For the purposes of this book, I'm going to help you setup a cold hardware wallet so that you can safely store your coins securely. (Another form of cold wallet is to store your coin keys on paper – not my preferred method)

It is vitally important to put your hardware wallet in a safe and secure place that you will remember. You definitely don't want to lose your investments like you could any old USB stick, right?

Setting up a hardware wallet is easy, but first of all where do you buy one? Simple! Amazon now carries the Ledger Nano S and the Trezor! Both wallets are very good and recommended.

The advantages of one over the other depend greatly on the firmware version as both are continually developing their products to accept more and more coins. I'm currently using the Nano S myself.

Here is a simple walkthrough of how to setup your hardware wallet:

1). Plug your wallet into the USB port on your computer, and follow the instructions on the wallet screen. You can choose to create a new wallet, or import a Bitcoin account or an Ethereum account (Litecoin and others are included too). Whatever your selection, you just need to observe the on-screen instructions all along the process, selecting and validating with the buttons on your wallet.

2.) Choose and memorize a PIN code that will be requested each time you connect your wallet. Confirm this PIN code and be careful to remember it as you could reset the wallet by inputting the wrong PIN code into it repeatedly.

3.) If equipped with a recovery phrase, copy on the "Recovery sheet" supplied in the box the 24 words in order of appearance. This step is really important to guarantee you can recover anytime your wallet in case of loss or theft. You won't be able to finish the configuration without confirming you copied the 24 words by selecting some of them as requested. Keep your "Recovery sheet" in a safe place.

4.) Once you've seen the mention: "Your device is now ready", your wallet is configured. Now you just have to install the Apps on your computer to use your wallet. In your Chrome browser, download for free the Ledger Wallet Bitcoin Chrome app or the Ledger Wallet Ethereum Chrome app. It only takes a few seconds for these apps to install.

5.) Now you can use your wallet with your Chrome apps on any computer, even a compromised one, to send or receive payments. Each transaction will be verified on the embedded display, and validated with buttons.

Once you receive the hardware wallet in the mail, you will go through the above steps to have to set it up using multi-factor authentication (MFA).
This is very good for security but also means that you'll need to either remember all of the code words applied as well as your PIN code or have them readily accessible in another secure location. (Fireproof safe, perhaps?)

Next, you will want to verify the address of your device.

This address is very important, it will be where you are sending and receiving your coins from. Absolutely no typos here, and I would recommend doing a dry run of sending coins first where you maybe send $2 across just to make sure you have the address typed in correctly. (Image 6 shows the menu)

Now how do you send coins to your wallet with this address? Head back over to Coinbase, log into your account and select the coin you would like to send first ($2 first to test this out). Here you will select the amount of coins you wish to send (either in USD or amount of coins themselves) and then you input the address of your wallet.

Once you have triple-checked the address and amounts, simply click on send. Now you will be treated to history in the making! You see, none of these transactions are going to be instant.

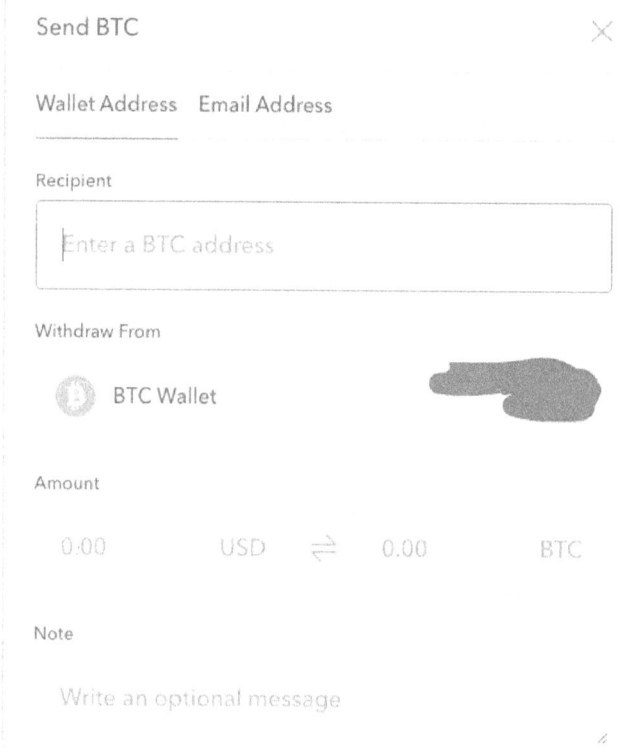

Send BTC   ✕

Wallet Address   Email Address

Recipient

Enter a BTC address

Withdraw From

    BTC Wallet

Amount

0.00   USD   ⇌   0.00   BTC

Note

Write an optional message

(Image 6 - Input your wallet address in the recipient field.)

I've completed Bitcoin transfers in roughly 20-40 minutes depending on network congestion, but also because you will now be watching your transfer be cleared by 6 different verification steps done automatically by the network.

After six confirmations, you will see that the transaction has cleared and is now available in your wallet. Congratulations, your coins are now safe! (Well, kind of…make sure you've got them all backed up on your wallet and disconnect the wallet using good USB stick procedure).

With your wallet in a secure spot, you can rest assured that your entire collection of coins (or partial if you want to keep some on the exchanges for trading or payments), are safe.

This is also a good method to help you with keeping your emotions in check when prices fluctuate and it allows you to hold onto your coins for that much longer since you now have to send your coins back to an exchange in order to use them. This dovetails nicely into Chapter 9, some trading strategies you can use with your coins.

Coinbase now offers online wallet storage for all 3 coins and there are a plethora of sites claiming to offer online storage for coins across the Internet. After Mt. Gox and different hacks of large corporations, I simply would not trust any online storage of coins and neither should you. Remember, we all thought our credit reports were safe too.

Hardware wallets have several advantages over wallets offered online:

1). You are in **physical possession** of your own coins at all times.

2). **No one can remotely hack** your wallet hidden in a secure space.

3). You have **complete control** over who accesses your wallet and coins.

4). There is **no risk of an insider threat** at one of the exchanges stealing user's coins with a hardware wallet.

5). It's **portable** and can be used on even a compromised computer.

6). It's **safe and secure**, with multifactor authentication preventing others from using your hardware wallet unattended.

7). It **does not require an Internet connection** to access your coins.

Lastly, the most important reason: You have access to your coins 24x7x365 with no service outages or interruptions and no risk of online theft.

If you plan to invest a lot of money, you would be putting yourself at a huge risk by not storing your coins offline. Just buy a hardware wallet; it saves you a lot of worrying in the long run. You won't find a better way of storing your coins privately and securely.

Chapter 8: How to Mine Coins

This chapter requires you to have a working knowledge of computer systems, specifically computer hardware. If you would rather not get into this level of detail as a beginner, then feel free to skip to the next chapter. I will be writing a short book on mining in the future based on the contents of this chapter. If you're still with me, let's look at some of the subjects related to mining crypto-currencies (mostly Bitcoin in this chapter).

During the emergence of Bitcoin, some people focused on trying to mine the coins themselves. By mining your own coins, you wouldn't need an exchange to pay for any new coins, you would just earn them. Since those early days of mining, there have been a lot of advancements and I will try to capture a few here.

Back in 2009, you could use your normal desktop computer to mine Bitcoin. At the time, the calculations to mine Bitcoin were still relatively quick to do and they did not require much computing power to accomplish. In fact, people just simply used the CPU (Central Processing Unit) processing power on their personal computer.

You would be able to mine entire blocks within a day and I've seen people mentioning that at the time, you could earn 50 Bitcoins in one day! Ah, the good old days.

As Bitcoin grew and more people started to mine coins, it became harder and harder to run the calculations on a normal desktop computer. This lead people to up the computing power and start to invest in something called a GPU (Graphics Processing Unit).

A GPU is a beefed up gaming video card that could then do the Bitcoin calculations 50-100 times faster than the regular CPUs could. It's essentially your video card in your computer, except for mining you will want one that is much more powerful than what typically comes in consumer-grade desktops and laptops.

The ability to rely solely on GPUs lasted until roughly 2014, when surprise surprise, computers became faster again and the difficulty of mining one Bitcoin again increased. This latest increase has seen the rise of another kind of technology to power the calculations required for Bitcoin farming.

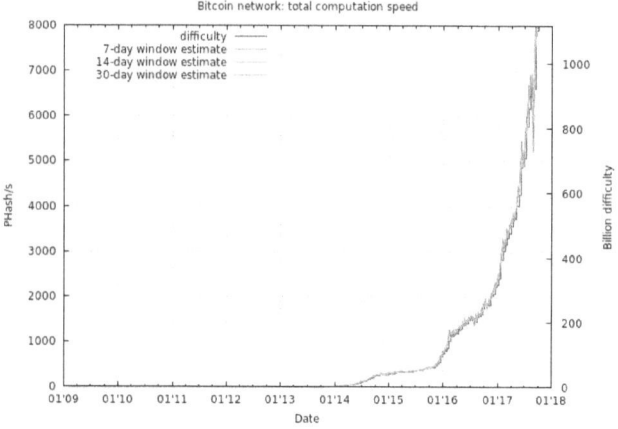

(Image 7 - As you see, the difficulty to mine Bitcoin has increased greatly)

Around late 2015, early 2016, the difficulty to mine Bitcoin started its ascent and (much like its price), grew at a tremendous rate putting it way beyond the ability for a CPU or GPU to mine a coin.

So what is needed these days to mine Bitcoin? Simple, it requires cheap electricity (preferably free electricity) and a rack of devoted ASIC-based computers.

ASIC-based computers are the newest wave in technology, capable of running the complicated equations needed to develop the digital signatures within each Bitcoin.

ASIC is an acronym that stands for **A**pplication-**S**pecific **I**ntegrated **C**ircuit, a more powerful type of processing unit. This technology takes an integrated circuit and then customizes it for a particular use (mining Bitcoin). An ASIC –based computer is super focused, super fast and super efficient at creating Bitcoins, but it's also more expensive. To build an ASIC-based rig, you are currently looking at spending upwards of $300 into the tens of thousands.

So how do people become miners and be profitable at doing it? Well, it's a case of math. First, you'll need to calculate what your kWh costs at your location. Then, you'll need to calculate how many bitcoins you will produce per hour using the ASIC rig. You will also need to know how much hashing power is required (also called the hash rate). The hash rate is the measuring unit of the processing power of the Bitcoin network. The Bitcoin network must make intensive mathematical operations for security purposes. When the network reached a hash rate of 10 Th/s, it meant it could make 10 trillion calculations per second.

Remember, to do these calculations, it consumes a lot of electricity. Image 7 below is a sample of how you can calculate whether or not this is feasible for you to do yourself:

	PROFIT RATIO PER DAY	PROFIT PER MONTH
	23%	$ 26.66

Calculated for 1 BTC = $ 4358.54	Profit per day $ 0.8888 Day	฿ 0.001058	$ 3.72
Hashing Power 4730 GH/s	Profit per week $ 6.22 Week	฿ 0.007408	$ 26.07
Power consumption (W) 1293	Profit per month $ 26.66 Month	฿ 0.03175	$ 111.72
Cost per KW/h ($) 0.12	Profit per year $ 324.40 Year	฿ 0.3863	$ 1,359.20

Calculators (and information on ASIC rigs for purchase) can be found on sites like **https://www.cryptocompare.com** and **https://www.coinish.com**. I recommend looking at both to learn more about calculating your profitability with your current electricity costs as well as ROI. Unless you want to run a massive farm, as you see in the example above, there is not a huge profit to make off of one miner alone. I wanted to include that example to show how much is required to understand before you choose to get into Bitcoin mining.

Now, let's say you want to mine a different coin than Bitcoin because the difficulty of mining Bitcoin is so high and expensive. Well, you have several options (due to all of the coins available).

The first easy option is to pick up the mining software for your coin of choice, which you can find on Google and then look into the hardware requirements (hashing power, kwh, power consumption), determine your return on investment (ROI) and purchase the hardware.

For example, if you are looking to mine a smaller coin like LTC, it doesn't require as much hashing power so your hardware costs will be cheaper.

(Image 8 - A Bitcoin mining "farm")

Mining is a topic that can be written in a book by itself, as there are many different ways that it can be done.

In this section I've covered it at a high level if you were looking to purchase a miner for yourself and mine Bitcoin. There are multiple other avenues to explore in mining beyond just this.

For starters, you can mine other coins and it will cost you less money up front. You can also buy into what is referred to as a miner pool. This is where several miners are pooling their resources together to mine more coins at less cost with the intent of making a higher ROI than if they mined alone.

The miner pool is a way to make returns from mining and diversify the returns due to different mining capabilities and costs. It also provides you with more computing power than trying to mine by yourself since you have multiple miners going at the same time.

The Crypto Compare website is excellent for helping you decide on which mining pool makes the most sense as they rank the different mining pools based on fees and expected returns.

One other avenue to investigate if you are interested in mining coins is to look at a company like Genesis Mining. Genesis Mining uses cloud computing to mine coins. This means that users buy the output of mining power from mining hardware placed in remote data centers. These remote data centers then do all of the mining remotely in the cloud.

What are the advantages to cloud mining vs. local mining? Less cost up front. With cloud mining you don't have to actually own any of the mining rigs yourself, you simply pay into the service and receive the mining output. The returns by doing this are lower, but it is banking on the fact that coin values continue to rise, which means that even if what you make today is only worth .00001 of a Bitcoin, in five years that value would be worth much more.

Now that you have a higher level of understanding around what goes into mining, what you'll need to mine, how to calculate your returns, and how you can become a miner, I'd like to go through some basic steps you can use to get started in mining.

Step 1: Purchase a Bitcoin (or your choice of coin) miner.

- Popular Bitcoin-mining hardware brands include AntMiner, BPMC, GekkoScience, TerraHash, and more.
- A Bitcoin mining machine can cost anywhere from a few hundred dollars to tens of thousands based on the hash rate.

Step 2: Purchase a hardware wallet

- We go over this in Chapter 7

Step 3: Decide on joining a pool, cloud mining or doing it on your own

- There are advantages to each, but this is up to you. I'd start off going at it alone just to learn how to calculate profitability and see if it's worth scaling up locally.
- If the ROI does not work out in your favor, then you may be interested in joining a pool or cloud mining group.

Step 4: Download a mining program

- Mining programs are almost always free and the program you select is based on the hardware you chose to mine with.

- Be sure to connect your wallet to the mining program so that all coins mined go directly to you. The same goes for if you connect to a mining pool or group. Connect your wallet to your account to receive the deposits.

- Configure the mining software on your computer. It will most likely operate from the command line and be an open source batch file. This step will vary based on the hardware/software that you select.

Step 5: Run the Mining Program

- After everything is configured and your wallet is connected, load the miner and begin mining.

- You may notice the computer slow to a crawl but that is why you aren't using your personal desktop to do the mining, right?

Step 6: Keep an eye on progress

- Make sure that the computer temperatures are within a safe range as it's running to prevent any hardware failures over time. A good safe range for mining hardware is below 175 degrees.
- Verify that coins are being generated and being placed in your wallet. You want to make sure that you have configured the miner correctly and the coins are going to the right address before you lose out on your hard work.

I hope this outline helps you in your journey to become a miner. As mentioned, these basic steps will work for any coin, not just Bitcoin, so feel free to investigate more into what hardware fits within your budget and electricity costs. This is a moving target as difficulty, mining payout and of course coin values all change with time, so while this chapter hasn't been exhaustive, it is meant to give you enough knowledge to at least understand the subject before delving into the hardware specs and electricity costs to run your own farm.

Never forget that as a miner, you will be in an arms race versus mining farms that are going to have the best hardware available to maximize their profit.

This means that from time to time, you may have to reinvest into better hardware. You will also want to make sure that you have the latest software updates and firmware as they are released for your mining program. This is an easy thing to do and check while you are configuring the device to run.

There are miners available for USB ports now, so this is an expanding field more and more people are getting invested into. While the outputs of these USB devices are very low, it still can amount to essentially "free" crypto-currency that you can earn in the background while you focus on other tasks around the house.

While the days of mining cheaply using just about any computer have largely gone by the wayside as competition has increased, it can be still be a personally rewarding experience with a small amount of technical savvy.

You may never become a millionaire from mining at your home, but there is always a benefit to learning a new skill and while the monetary gains may not translate, you'll still have essentially earned coins out of nothing. Unlike printing dollar bills at home, mining your own coins is also not highly illegal.

So you've now learned what crypto-currency is, how it's used, which coins are available, how to setup an account to buy, sell and send it, how to safely store it and now how to mine it. The next question is…how do you trade it?

Chapter 9: Crypto Trading Strategies:

It's important to say right up front that any advice given in this section is not professional, is entirely your decision to follow and any gains or losses are solely your own and no responsibility lies with me. (Although if you make a huge profit, I will gladly accept donations!)

Before delving entirely into this topic, let's pull back and take a macro view of crypto-currency on a few factors. The first factor that needs to be said is that we are on the cusp of either widespread acceptance of Bitcoin, a compelling use case for Ethereum, or a breakthrough with Litecoin for everyday small and quick transactions. To date none of this has happened yet.

However, it is important to continually pull back the lens and look at this from the perspective of 1994 Internet. Bitcoin has only been around since 2009 and has seen rapid growth over the past 3 years. Prior to then, the momentum was steady, but it was slow. All crypto-coins have taken awhile to gain value, with a few explosions; the general trend is a slow climb up over years.

This slow climb is where I base my projections and why I'm not going to tell you what you should do since every situation is personal. What I can impart is that if you believe in blockchain technology and believe in decentralized money that is digital in nature and has the advantages that crypto-currency can bring to the table, you will find a compelling reason to invest with a long term strategy and view.

Remember – This is the natural technological progression from rocks, minerals to paper to digital. It's coming regardless of what people say, the only question is who will be there early enough to make large profits from it. If you've picked up this book and followed along with me so far, then you are an early adopter who will make money in the crypto-currency markets.

If you prefer to make money quicker, then crypto has ample opportunities available with the hundreds of smaller coins out there to turn double-digit jumps and allow people to short the market for rapid turnarounds in profits and losses.

This short term gain is not the purpose of this book, but plenty of money can be made doing it provided you know what you are doing and can accept a high level of risk.

For short-term gains and action, I recommend following the principles of Technical Analysis to be sure you aren't selling at the bottom or buying at the top.

The biggest mistake I have seen people make in stocks and now crypto-coins is doing exactly this.

They will see Bitcoin approaching $5,000 and go all-in, then when it drops down to $2900, they will sell based off of fear, unknown and doubt (FUD). When trading anything dealing in markets, you must always maintain your sobriety and never let emotions get in the way of a good trade.

Short term vs. Long term is your own personal decision on an emerging technology like Crypto-currency.

People take losses in every market by trying to time the market and guessing wrong. As I've seen with day trading crypto, trading the chops (when the coin goes up and down within a small percentage repeatedly) is a very hard thing to do correctly and it often results in losses.

Other people play it correctly enough to add to their holdings. Some short calls are right in sight and easy to pull off with some patience if you recognize what the chart is telling you through sound Technical Analysis (TA) principals.

If you are familiar with charts, I've included some patterns on the next page to get a sense of what is about to happen, based on the chart patterns.

Reversal Patterns

Double Top
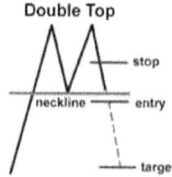

Head and Shoulders
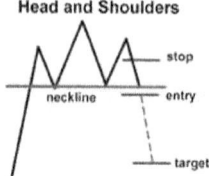

Rising Wedge
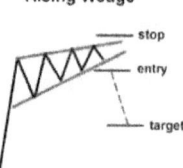

Double Bottom
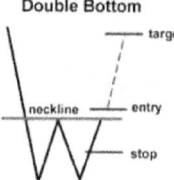

Inverse Head and Shoulders
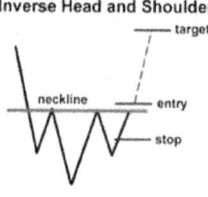

Falling Wedge
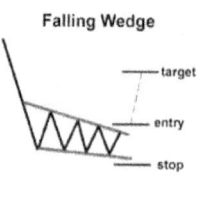

Continuation Patterns

Falling Wedge
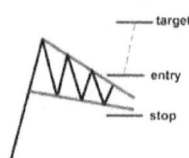

Bullish Rectangle
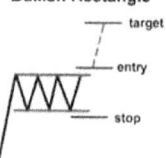

Bullish Pennant
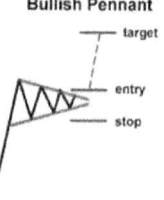

Rising Wedge
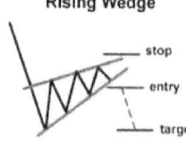

Bearish Rectangle
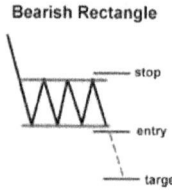

Bearish Pennant
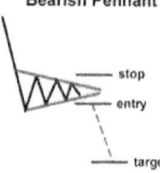

Bilateral Patterns

Ascending Triangle
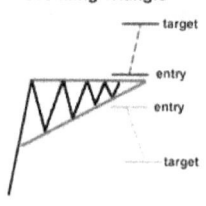

Descending Triangle
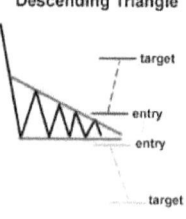

Symmetrical Triangle
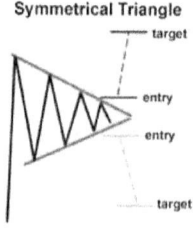

It's important to note that we have seen extreme changes within the crypto-coins value in under a month. Since the crypto-markets are open 24 hours a day, seven days a week worldwide, you see price fluctuations rapidly. Think about it this way: You have over twice as many working hours in crypto-trading as you do trying to trade the regular stock market in each day. This means that when short term trading, you can't make guesses on developing patterns within a short window like 15 minutes. It means next to nothing most of the time. You'll want to pull back your view to 60 minutes at the least to help guide you in terms of where the market could be heading. With so many people involved across the world, it makes it hard to accurately predict more than 3 hours ahead, and that is reserved to the people who know what they're looking at after years of trading. This is all said not to dissuade you from day trading crypto, but more to serve as a guide for what to look out for and what to keep in mind before you set your limits and start shorting coins.

What these patterns are showing you are ways to look at the patterns on your chart for each coin and attempt to predict which direction the coin is going in. These are going to be very familiar to you if you've traded stocks before.

Overall, I'm not sure you can go entirely wrong either way you play it (short term or long term), but based on the historical gains and technological momentum, my own money is on the long-term strategy working out for the major 3 coins.

Long-term strategy:

With the tax rates in the US, it makes sense to hold onto investments for at least one year due to capital gains tax (which we went over in Chapter 4). If you play it short, you'll need to make enough to cover the additional tax burden. If you play it long, you get to keep more of your earnings provided the coins continue to rise in value.

With Coinbase, you aren't given a robust trading platform; it's more the vehicle you can use to get into the market rather than to play it. I would recommend looking into other services that are out there like Bittrex, Polyniex or GDAX if you're so inclined. Bittrex currently seems to be the best platform for trading due to the capabilities and options that it includes.

As someone who doesn't currently day trade, I can't speak to the functionality for playing the market, but I do know that it is a very popular platform due to the variety of coins that it has along with the toolsets provided. So with the different services that exist, you have to decide if you're in crypto for the daily play or if this is a long-term stash and hold. Only you can answer that for yourself.

For the long-term strategy, I prefer to rely upon buying in during the dips in price and holding. Holding onto your coins and then also adding to your position over time is the best way to traditionally build value as well as increase your wealth in stable stocks.

While coins are not stocks, it's important to think of them as another vehicle for your future wealth.

By holding onto Bitcoin, Litecoin, Ethereum you can hedge with which one becomes the mainstream market go-to after the public use case expands to where crypto-currency becomes more involved in people's regular lives. This is also very effective because it let's you add to your position over time when the crypto market has its inevitable dips. For example, Bitcoin recently touched $4800 back in August 2017. It then swung downwards, as low as $2800, before starting to climb back up to it's current $4300 valuation. If you were holding during this time, you would not want to cash out, but rather you would be looking to add at the lower prices!

I am a big supporter of the holding strategy for a few reasons which I will list on the next page.

1.) Crypto-coins have risen in value since 2009

2.) Crypto-coins are gaining acceptance in new markets, not losing it

3.) Crypto-coins continue to adopt new technologies to improve performance and usability

With these three factors, it's apparent that this technology isn't just going to go away on its own. Your investment reasoning may take into account other variables that I haven't mentioned or even thought of (!) but it's important to note these three for why a holding strategy is less likely to fail than investing in random penny stocks for example. It's also important to mention that with institutional investors starting to get into crypto-currency, there will be a flood of money coming in that can raise the market caps drastically very quickly.

It's time for the "past performance does not predict future value" portion of the trading strategy section of this book. There are risks associated with this. If you only read news headlines, you may have even heard the term "bubble" being thrown around when it comes to Bitcoin, etc. While none of us can say whether that is true or not, what I can say is that if you look at the market caps of Bitcoin, Litecoin and Ethereum, you would see that there is more money tied into several Fortune 100 companies by themselves.

Could the market cap of crypto all disappear overnight? I'm very confident in saying that's not going to happen. I'd venture to say that's unlikely, especially as adoption of these coins as payment platforms continues to increase along with the usage of Bitcoin to be a store of value rises.

Will it be the next Pets.com or the next Amazon? You can decide for yourself, but from where I'm sitting, it looks like money to be had if you get in before the mainstream. In fact, I might even guarantee that that is the case with crypto-currency. Since it is decentralized, no government or one entity can come along and kill it. You would see a massive outpouring of news and have plenty of red flags before the entire blockchain system collapsed. (And this is highly improbable due to how distributed the network truly is).

As with all things related to investments, it's important to view things with the macro lens and not get too caught up in the day-to-day activities that can drive a news cycle.

I have seen people lose a lot of money by playing with market timing and trying to guess which chart predicts where the value of coins will be next.

Due to this, my suggestion for the long term holding strategy is probably the safest one, but there will always be someone claiming to have beat the system with their technique or skill level. It's up to you whether to believe in them or not.

This does not take away from solid fundamentals, technical analysis or having a good view to what problem each coin is attempting to solve. You will also have to keep up to date with the changes that the development team for each coin is planning on.

This is just like investing in the stock of a company. You will want to check in regularly to ensure that your money is being put to good use. Sometimes, you may have to sell at a loss to protect yourself from losing everything. This is another reason why researching into your choice is an absolute must.

As we've seen with Initial Coin Offerings (remember, ICOs?), there are some real scam coins that exist, so it is up to you to make sure your long-term investments have solid objective reasons behind them. Luckily, the main 3 coins in this book all have just that.

Now are you interested in a strategy for day trading crypto-coins? Great! I highly recommend that you follow the appropriate day traders on twitter. I've listed some in Chapter 12.

They know far more than I do about that realm and even though they do get things wrong from time to time, there are a lot of people day trading and not needing to work a 9-5 anymore because of how good they've gotten at it.

With crypto-currency, this is a round the clock venture every day of the week. It can make for wild swings based on rumors or news that otherwise wouldn't occur on the stock market. It's important to protect yourself with stop loss limits and also to not overexpose yourself on shorts with this kind of market. I would recommend a more conservative approach with your trading in crypto just because of its inherent volatility. Peaks are greater than normal stocks, but the dips are also deeper.

Be careful!

Now, you're all mentally prepared to get into trading and you have your Coinbase account setup. Let's walk you through setting up an account on one of the trading exchanges. For this, I'm going to walk you through signing up to Bittrex. I'm a big fan of this site because of its features, coin offerings and use of two-factor authentication for access into your account. It'll also maintain a time limit on an inactive window so that you will get logged out for your safety if you have to leave your computer for any reason.

To start, you're going to want to head over to **https://www.bittrex.com**
To sign up, you will need an email address and a password.
(See Image 9 on next page)

BITTREX

SIGN UP

> E-mail address

> Password

> Confirm Password

☐ I agree to the Bittrex.com Terms of Service

&+ SIGN UP

Already have an account? Sign in

(Image 9 – the welcome screen to Bittrex)

After you provide those details, you will get an email walking you through the registration process.

Download the Google Authenticator app onto your smart phone and add the Bittrex hash icon so that you are able to access the account in the future.

Once you confirm the details around your identity such as name, birth date and address, you will have a Basic account. A Basic account is limited to 3 Bitcoins (BTC) per day in withdrawals. I suggest also adding your phone number and verifying it through the site as well for Phone Verification. This is important should you ever get locked out of the account.

The next step is for Enhanced Verification and it is what will allow you to trade large limits on the platform. I highly recommend doing this if you plan on withdrawing greater than 100 BTC or equivalent per day.

Tips for successful verification:

- Take a fresh selfie, ensure nothing is blocking a full view of your face
- Do not use the same image from your identification documents
- Do not use a professional profile picture
- Do not manipulate the image of your identification in anyway. This includes

adding watermarks or blacking out
certain information
- Do not crop the image of your ID such
that any portion of the ID is removed
including edges

(Bittrex recommends this for Enhanced Verification)

Once you have an account setup with Bittrex,
you will need to send some Bitcoin to your
Bittrex account. To do this, login back into
your Coinbase account on your desktop and
click Accounts. From this screen, you will see
your current Bitcoin holdings and a button
directly underneath that says Send.
This step is identical to what you do to send
coins to your hardware wallet! The only
difference is that the receiving address is
going to be your Bittrex account address.

To find the account address in your Bittrex account head back to Bittrex and click on the Wallets key in the top header menu (Image 10).

(Image 10)

Then you will be in your Account Balances page. Go down to BTC in the first table listing and click on the plus (+) button next to the BTC row:

This will then pop up the address menu for you to send your BTC from Coinbase.

DEPOSIT BITCOIN (BTC)

I acknowledge the following information: By depositing tokens to this address, you agree to our deposit recovery policy. Depositing tokens to this address other than BTC may result in your funds being lost.

Address   1HWkYogN8oV6HfFpXW2XgZnr8W3YoZQhua   ADDR

Depositing tokens to this address other than BTC will result in your funds being lost.

Once you have this address, copy it, return to Coinbase, click the Send button under your BTC holdings and you'll see this:

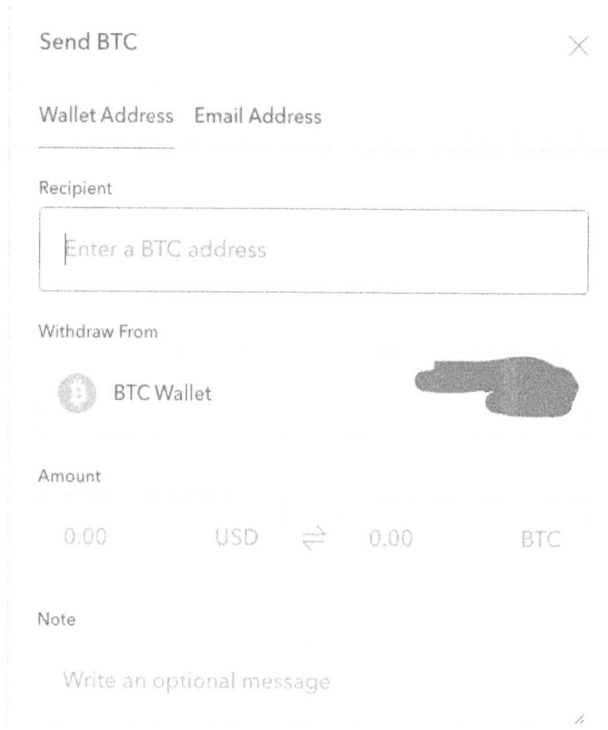

Send BTC

Wallet Address   Email Address

Recipient

Enter a BTC address

Withdraw From

BTC Wallet

Amount

0.00   USD   ⇌   0.00   BTC

Note

Write an optional message

Paste the address from Bittrex in the Recipient field and then enter in the amounts you'd like to send.

From there, you will go through 6 verifications of the transaction between Coinbase and Bittrex. Grab a coffee or drink during this time because I have waited as long as 40 minutes before the Bitcoin appeared in my Bittrex account.

Do not be alarmed that the coins are lost! As long as you put in the address correctly, let Coinbase, the public ledger and Bittrex do their thing.

Now that you have BTC in your Bittrex account, you are ready to start trading! Head over to the top menu:

Click on Markets

Sort By:	Volume		Max Rows: 3		Search:		
XRP	0.00005504	8.7% ↑	NEO	0.00744998	0.6% ↑
ADA	0.00000498	-4.2% ↓	OMG	0.00202503	-1.2% ↓
EMC2	0.00001769	-12.8% ↓	XLM	0.00000337	19.9% ↑

Click on any of the coins you're interested in, I clicked on XRP for this example:

Image 16 - What is that chart telling you? (Look at the patterns page)

Now, let's say we would like to buy some XRP with our Bitcoins. Scroll down and go here (Image 17):

TRADING

BUY RIPPLE				1E-8 BTC AVAILABLE
Units	Max		0.00000000	XRP
Bid	Price ▾		0.00000000	BTC
Type	Limit ▾	Time In Force	Good 'Til Cancelled ▾	‹
			What is this?	
Total	฿		0.00000000	BTC

+ Buy Ripple

(Image 17)

This is where things get fun. Select how much XRP you would like to buy, then what type of buy you'd like: Limit (on by default), or Conditional. Then set the transaction as Immediate or Cancel, or Good 'Til Cancelled. This allows you to have some control over how much you're buying and when.
Initiate the buy and you're the proud owner of an alt coin!

If you would like to sell your alt coins, then go right next to the Sell menu here (Image 18):

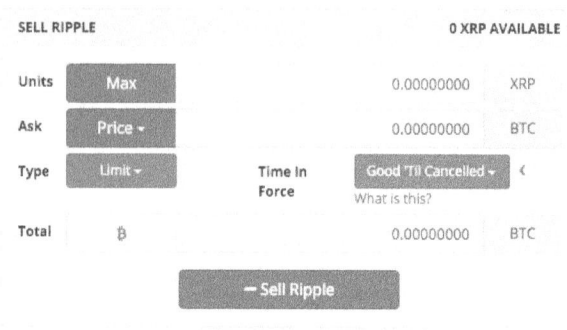

(Image 18)

Selling is very similar to buying in Bittrex. The sold coins will then appear in BTC in your Account Balances, which you access through this Wallets button (Remember?)

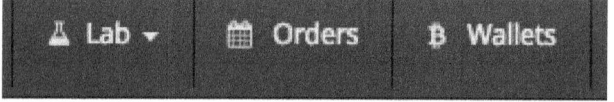

You now have a Bittrex account setup and know how to send BTC to it, navigate the menus, as well as use BTC to buy and sell alt coins.

Congratulations, you can now trade coins!

Throw in some Technical Analysis on the coin charts and you too can be a day trader in crypto!

Ok, some parts of this are definitely missing, such as setting stop loss limits as well as a myriad of other features and functions that a powerful site such as Bittrex can offer people.

If you know how to day trade, a lot of the functions of this site will feel familiar, especially if you are coming from a platform like eTrade.

If this is all new to you, then I would recommend you reach out for advice from the day trader groups on twitter (which I'll mention some good follows in the additional resources section of this book) so that you can interact with experienced crypto traders and learn from the ground up.

This is a rewarding investment and with time and energy, you may soon be spotting the trends and making some quick money off of the crypto market.

The expectation of making money is why you first purchased this book and while I've talked about all the features and functions of coins, markets and websites, I haven't told you where to expect prices to go.

Let's make that prediction on the next page.

Chapter 10: Future Forecasts

One of the most popular questions that I see (almost daily) is what will X coin be worth in X time. Since time travel has yet to be invented (I'm looking at you, Elon Musk), this game of predicting is full of bad guesses, but there are also some intelligent, educated and reasoned guesses out there that are based on technical analysis. I will attempt to do something in-between these guesses using what I've seen thrown about by people with track records in crypto.

This section will also be very fun to look back at in a few years, if only to see just how wrong I was about the different values. We may not even be talking about coin values in that future period, so take all of this with a grain of salt.

The first coin to forecast is of course, the big one: Bitcoin. Bitcoin has had some amazing values thrown about with the media hype that has occurred surrounding it. The safest bet I have seen with Bitcoin is a $5,000 valuation per coin by the end of 2017. That is a safe number that feels right after seeing the coin hit $4800 back in August. However, I think that you're looking for something a little further out than end of 2017. My prediction for Bitcoin's price by 2020 is going to be less than the $100,000 prediction or the $1,000,000 prediction by 2025 that I've seen from John McAfee.

For 2020, I would expect Bitcoin to be worth $12,000 a coin.

Here is why: We have seen Bitcoin's growth to have exploded this past year from $900 in March up to $4800, but then hit real resistance and dip hard back down to $2800. This is all before we start to see the institutional money come in. How much will that institutional money be worth? Well, let's look at the market cap of Bitcoin as of September 2017. It is currently valued at $64,839,560,873 per coinmarketcap.com. $64 billion sounds like a lot of money, but compared to many companies on the Fortune 100, it is a sliver.

For example, the value of Microsoft's market cap is $564 billion. That is over $500 billion more in one company than Bitcoin's entire worth!

Bitcoin at $12,000 would be equivalent of a $195 billion market cap, which is less than half that of Microsoft alone but would show a 3x growth rate in less than 3 years.

That's also figuring in another economic recession over the next 18 months in the U.S.

Some may look at this prediction and scoff; others may think it'll be even higher. Both can be correct by 2020. It's important to note that while there is a lot of momentum in Bitcoin's direction, it could also be the MySpace to another coin's Facebook and be worthless in 2020. This is HIGHLY doubtful, but such is life in technology!

For Litecoin, I'm looking at the upcoming technological enhancements, what has already been implemented and how tied it is to Bitcoin's value.

Litecoin today is massively undervalued at $52 a coin, and has already seen a peak of $98 a coin. Many expect Litecoin to hit $100 by the end of 2017, and I'd venture a guess at $120 by the end of 2017 only because if it retraces $98, it shouldn't stop at $100.

For 2020, I would expect that due to Bitcoin's growth and the usage of atomic swaps, Litecoin will be even more popular and a solid $500-$1,000 range could be the right target for it's value.

Make no mistake, this is a solid currency that has real upside for more but with 4x the supply of Bitcoin, it will not command the same price premium as Bitcoin does for a long time (if ever).

The advantage of Litecoin has been that despite the dip, it's generally the most stable of all crypto-currencies to date in that the price doesn't have wild fluctuations.

It is a good coin to park some of your investment, as it will continue to grow in value at a stable, solid rate.

Litecoin has several advantages for being the crypto-currency that is used in small transactions day to day, like buying a cup of coffee. This may also limit the amount it becomes priced at, since a large valuation may shy away people from investing in it and consuming it.

That gets into psychology a little bit, but it's something to keep in the back of your mind. Everyday small transactions are meant to be cheap, so why shouldn't the coin be?

I hope that I'm wrong about this as I do have holdings in LTC, but I've seen a lot of sideways action recently and my long-term prospects for this coin range from promising to mixed. That is why a $500-$1,000 valuation comes in when Bitcoin is $12,000. I just don't know if people will flip over to Litecoin for all of their consumption purchasing.

 If they do, then the upside is massive. It is still definitely a coin to keep in your portfolio for stable future growth, but keep an eye on it.

Ethereum is the wild card and that is why I put it last. This is a platform that has traded at $400 before dipping down below $200 during the large dip in September. Ethereum has the open source blockchain capability with applications being written based off of it, which means it could have multiple uses all beyond the use of a simple currency.

With that said, it becomes hard to predict where the valuation will be in 2020. By the end of this year, I would expect it to return to the $350 range since rising waters raise all ships and the crypto market is slowing recovering from the large sell-off that occurred during the beginning of September. Ethereum packs a lot of future promise and while it has its challenges with development and releases, it is a strong player for "coin that could replace Bitcoin". Its use of smart contracts adds a dimension to the blockchain that Bitcoin could not match.

Its development has spawned several new teams looking to build platforms and other coins off of its ledger and off of clone ledgers in order to speed up transactions.

The 2020 realm could be extremely good for Ethereum. One blockchain project takes off and it could be the next $3,000 "coin". With solid backing and a development team more than capable of implementing new enhancements to the technology, I would expect no lower than $1,500 for Ethereum by 2020.

Predictions can make people with the best intentions look like fools, so please don't base your entire investment strategy on this one data point. Do your own research and follow the trends that you see developing long after this book reaches print. While these guesses are all within the realm of possibility and some even quite likely, there are external events that can deeply impact a coin and it's future valuation.

I would pay attention to the charts and also to the news to make sure you have parked your investments in the right coins. I would also develop the working ability to transfer funds within the three areas I've outlined (Coinbase, wallet, Bittrex) so that you are able to maintain flexibility with buying power during the dips. Dips and Rises are natural occurrences of the crypto market and markets at large since the beginning of currency.

This leads us to want to know what to look out for when making our decisions so that we don't make a costly mistake. While dips have been severe, the macro lens will show a strong growth uptick after each dip, which means if you buy during the dips and hold during the rises, you will find yourself in a much better position than when you first started.

In fact, the next chapter will discuss more of what to look out for and what has happened this summer, which had a dramatic impact on valuation of these coins.

Before we go to that, let's just point out the obvious: The going belief of many is that these coins will all increase in value tremendously for early adopters.

Chapter 11: What to Look Out For

It is September 2017, and we have just witnessed both the extreme highs of crypto-currency investing as well as the extreme lows. These swings are quite real and while I've described them before, let me put this into numerical context as well as a timeline to show just how extreme it is. Crypto investing is not for the weak willed and never will be for people without patience. That means you cannot have weak hands and you must keep an eye to the long-term trend at all times when going through the bear markets.

On September 1st, Bitcoin crossed the long predicted $5,000 price per coin, reaching a maximum value of $5,013. Staying true to it silver formula to Bitcoin's gold, Litecoin hit it's all-time high of $98 per coin on September 1st as well.

Ethereum, continually on it's own valuation path, has yet to repeat its performance in June, when it was at it's all time high of $415 per coin.

What has happened since September 1? Currently, Bitcoin sits at $4,300 after a drop of over 40% (touching the $2890's at one point). Litecoin shrugged off the $98 almost as quickly as it hit it and dropped all the way down to $38 per coin before rising slowly back to it's current value of $52.

Ethereum shows good stability at the $290-300 mark, but dropped as low as the $190's during the Bitcoin crash.
So what the heck happened? Well first let's talk about the reactions of the general public and Wall Street during this time.

Early in August, Bitcoin was chugging along and flirting with $5,000. There was strong optimism in the market that crypto-currency was gaining exposure, new investors and higher valuations. This optimism carried press coverage with it and CNBC hopped onto the Bitcoin bandwagon and started to devote sections of its show to crypto-coins. Along with this increase in positive press about Bitcoin, there would be pushback with negative viewpoints expressed about the entire movement. None hit harder than the views expressed by Jaime Dimon of JP Morgan who stated that "Bitcoin "is a fraud" and it will "blow up"

Speaking at a bank investor conference in New York, Dimon said, "The currency isn't going to work. You can't have a business where people can invent a currency out of thin air and think that people who are buying it are really smart."

Dimon said that if any JPMorgan traders were trading the crypto-currency, "I would fire them in a second, for two reasons: It is against our rules and they are stupid, and both are dangerous."

To many investors in the crypto-movement, these comments were met with laughter and derision as JP Morgan had been bailed out in the financial crisis of 2008 (which ironically is what spawned the decentralized currency movement a la Bitcoin to begin with).

So finding Jaime Dimon as a critic didn't impact believers in crypto in the least, however it did sink the markets as mainstream money was scared off by his comments as well as the next large factor for the dip in coin valuation during September…China.

It started with a rumor and several half-confirmations, but finally it was official: China would ban ICOs, mining and crypto-currency trading. The crypto-market reacted with FUD (Fear, Uncertainty, Doubt) and all valuations tumbled dramatically. As you have seen the highs listed next to the current prices earlier, it has been quite a ride this month alone. Many people sold as the coins dropped or near the bottom, resulting in losses to their portfolio or at best, anxiety. The fear that this was a bubble after all crossed the minds of most new investors and the correction continued on for days.

During this time, you had three camps of investor strategies. The first investor sold off his crypto holdings after everything dropped 20-40%.

The second investor attempted to make day trades with shorts. The third investor held onto their current portfolio while making buys at discounted coin valuations.

Quiz-time, which one do you think was the proper one during a large correction?

If you answered the third one for 90% of people, then you are correct. While some day traders can play bear market corrections and the other inevitable market movements, most people will get burned.

As this happened, I kicked myself for not selling as the coins were nearing their all time highs. Live and learn. Since I can't trust myself with timing the market correctly, I held on for the bear run. This meant that crypto was dead to me for a few days as I let the market sort itself out. No checking the prices, no reading crypto-twitter and seeing the negativity. For me, not seeing the negativity and panic helped me maintain my patience and composure while others sold out of FUD.

As the market has begun to turn around, this holding strategy showed to be the wise move. Another thing that I did during this correction was to buy up as much crypto as I could while it was on discount!

Why am I telling you this? Because one of the biggest things you need to look out for in crypto are the emotional pulls to do what the majority is doing. You need to stay detached when things get bad and pay attention when things get really good. This means not checking Coinbase for price updates every five minutes as you watch your investments go down in value. It only breeds anxiety and panic, which are the two forces working against you as an investor.

If I could sum up the majority of questions that I've gotten since writing the first edition of this book, it would be summed up this way "Prices are tanking, I'm nervous, what should I do?" Well, let me tell you what you should do!
HOLD ONTO YOUR COINS. Let me repeat that one more time: HOLD ONTO YOUR COINS.

Ok great, now that you have agreed to not panic sell when the next bear market hits the crypto world (and they can come at anytime!), let's get into what you should do instead next time.

Next time you see price action across the board dropping due to negative news, remember to breathe. You have a portfolio of coins that has beaten the crap out of the stock market over the last year. This means that it is growing on a macro level by leaps and bounds. This also means that people are going to take advantage of these massive profits and sell off from time to time. Relax; this is all natural cycles of the market.

So, the market is tanking, you're holding on with tears in your eyes, guess what you should be doing?

BUYING MORE COINS. That's right! (Provided you've already stayed away from ICOs and scam coins). Now don't buy with all of your spare cash at once, because if you do that too soon, you may end up losing more as the market continues downward. What you should be doing instead is to place small incremental buys as the market goes down. I like to do 10% initially then ramp up as the market dip becomes deeper to 25%, then 40%, then the remaining amount.

This formula is not a rule or law, but I wanted to share how you can mitigate your losses while buying in a down market, and also setting yourself up for a higher rate of return once the market returns to bull season (and it will).

Now, you say this is all good theory, but you can't lose hundreds or thousands of dollars and not do anything about it. Breathe and then take a moment to look at this chart below:

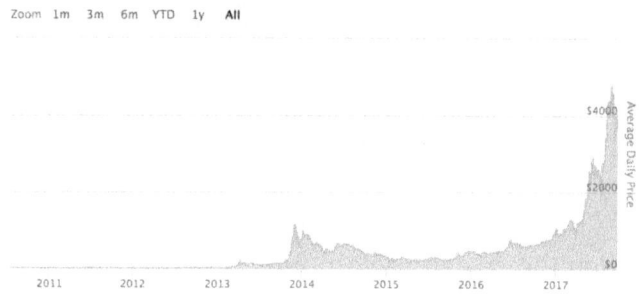

Look at it closely. Do you see the fluctuations in 2014? Do you see the peaks up followed by dips down? Now look at the trend with a linear line. Does it go up? Yes, it does. You can even cut 2017 out of the picture entirely and it will still be positive growth!

What I'm getting to is quite simply, do not panic and do not fear the bear market. It is as inevitable as the rotation of the Earth and if you buy in accordingly, you can continue to ride the waves to prosperity in crypto-coins.

Now, to shift this section into the positive: What else you should look out for?

Look for the widespread adoption of Bitcoin as a currency online, specifically by Amazon and other major retailers.

Rumors are swirling right now that Amazon will start to accept Bitcoin (just like Overstock.com) in the coming months. What this means for crypto is mainstream acceptance will be coming shortly afterwards!

Remember way back in this book when I showed you the technological lifecycle? We are in the early adopter phase right now, but if the rumors of Amazon accepting payments in Bitcoin become true, you will see the crypto-sphere start to become mainstream. As an investor, this is the moment that you've been waiting for. Widespread adoption of Bitcoin by the largest retailer in the Western world means that transactions and use cases for the coins will become much larger and much more common.

This means that Bitcoin could double in price within a week with the flood of new money coming into it! Remember the market cap I discussed in my projections? Keep in mind how small of a slice of the monetary pie a $190 billion market cap is. The entire world's currency is over $68 TRILLION.

Think that leaves Bitcoin with a little bit of room to grow? Now pair up with a retail giant such as AMAZON, think that the room for growth gets larger?

That's right, we are talking extreme growth here in the coming months and that is before Wall Street starts attaching crypto-currency funds to people's 401k plans. Goldman Sachs is rumored to be looking into Bitcoin for investments themselves. (You can't get more mainstream than that!)

More things to keep in mind with crypto: Widespread adoption of the coins will bring on additional retailers and consumer use cases for these coins. Once it appears on Amazon, you can be rest assured that Target, Wal-Mart, eBay and the regular cast of big box retailers will come online to support crypto-currency too!

There's more to consider with these three coins too. As you will see once you get more into crypto-news, software updates and enhancements to these coins is continually ongoing and it pays to pay attention to them. For example, the Bitcoin hard fork back on August 1st was the key driver behind the bull run that Bitcoin experienced during August. It led to the formation of an offshoot coin called Bitcoin Cash, which happened due to developers and miners choosing to not activate segwit on their mining operations.

THIS WAS GREAT FOR INVESTORS!

Not only did the price of their Bitcoin investment shoot up, but they also received the equivalent shares in Bitcoin Cash coins!

As this was a best-case scenario of a hard fork split, it helps to stay aware so that you can cash out your investments when you want to take some profit home with you. Hey, everybody wants a better life or else they wouldn't invest!

This chapter has become much longer than I intended but there is so much to relay to a new investor here. Always stay informed and keep an eye on what the coin development teams are working on. It allows you to make better decisions with your purchasing, holding and taking of profits when the time comes. It will also let you know which coins are worth investing in, as more and more ICOs pop up every week.

The problem with investing in crypto has been a separation of knowledge from the general public so far. Despite my attempts to educate everyone with the first edition of this book, vast swaths of the global population are not participating in this technological revolution yet.

This unfortunately will continue to separate the haves from the have not's further.
Please do your friends and family a favor and inform them of this trend (get them a copy of this book too!) just to help arm them with the knowledge they will need to get ahead of the game.

This crypto-coin movement is a lot like the iceberg that hit the Titanic. People see it from far away but don't avert it. Help them avert it and get them into the game. They will thank you later.

The future is bright and the dips are expected. Where else can you go to learn more about the various topics we have discussed in this book in more detail? Well, I've been searching around and have put together some additional resources that you can use, read, share and post about to drive some good conversations around crypto-currency and the market in general. The intent of this list was not to be all-inclusive, but rather to serve up some different areas of knowledge that line up with what we've discussed in this book so far.

The best thing about crypto-currency is that all of the information about it that is relevant can be found on the Internet with a lot of searching.

My intent has been to condense all of that information to save you time as well as provide you with the locations of resources that can help you grow as an investor and crypto-advocate. I did this so that you would be able to learn all of the basics in one place without needlessly sitting in front of a computer for days on end.

Your learning should not stop here and I'm going to provide you with several key resources in the next chapter that will allow you to gain more in-depth information on any of the topics that we have gone over in this book.

The different coins that make up crypto-currency all have their own support groups, fan clubs and news sites that you can follow.

It is important to know what your investments are doing so that you can plan accordingly. Since this is a 24x7x365 market, each week will bring with it a lot of news and headlines about each coin.

For example, right now with Bitcoin alone, I have seen at least 4 different articles in one morning about the November hard fork. If you ever wanted something to read, there is plenty with crypto-currency.

Without anymore delay, the chapter which can set you on the path to self-learning…

Chapter 12: Additional Resources

We've discussed nearly everything in this book at a level that should introduce you to the topics as well as provide the working knowledge you need to act on what you have learned. This working knowledge will lead you into areas where you will need more specific guidance, but be careful about what advice you find.

For a great background on Bitcoin and the origins of it, I would recommend the documentary on Netflix called <u>Banking on Bitcoin</u>. This will give you the story of Satoshi Nakamoto and some theories on who he could have been.

For a good overview of crypto-currency in general, you're holding it!

Other resources include:

https://www.cryptoinsider.com

https://www.cryptocoinsnews.com

https://www.coindesk.com

https://news.bitcoin.com

For information on Bitcoin mining, three sites I enjoy are:

https://www.coinish.com

https://www.cryptocompare.com

https://www.bitcoinmining.com

For information on Crypto taxes, here are two sites you should memorize:

https://www.irs.gov/newsroom/irs-virtual-currency-guidance

https://turbotax.intuit.com/tax-tools/tax-tips/Taxes-101/Tax-Tips-for-Bitcoin-and-Virtual-Currency/INF29402.html

For technical analysis information, the site I use is:

https://www.technicallycrypto.com

As always, check the charts and learn to identify patterns.
For fun, I also like to check social media accounts (Twitter especially). This is a collection of users that I personally follow and feel that they help provide positive contributions to the crypto community.

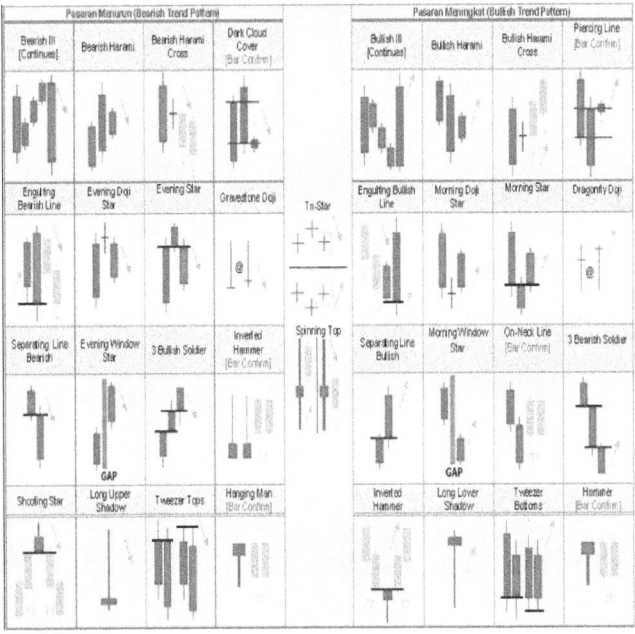

There are literally hundreds of accounts worth mentioning but to keep it short for space purposes, here are some random ones that offer good content.

@DM_BrooksCrypto

@TechnicalCrypto

@CharlieShrem

@CryptoNewsWire

@CryptoPikachu

@NicTrades

@Crypt0maniacs

@chryspto

@etcmining

@Crypto-Tube

@Beerdhead

@RealTimeCrypto

@PrecioBTC

After you follow these accounts, you'll start to see other people suggested and my recommendation is to follow most accounts associated with crypto. You may also find yourself laughing at the latest picture shared among the group above.

It's easy to gain insights and knowledge from the community into what's causing a market rise or dip, and if we are going to make a lot of money soon or just lose it all in one blip. (I'm kidding).

Develop your network with like-minded individuals and you'll eventually get the information you need quicker than the web sites will report it.

This will help you keep a step ahead with your trades, buys and sells. It's not insider trading, but it's definitely an advantage, which you should take full use of in the crypto game!

I wouldn't be where I am now with my crypto portfolio, earnings and other benefits from this journey if it weren't for the vast amount of information already out there and people willing to teach new joiners to the crypto world.

It's important to share the knowledge and pass it on because there is so much upside left to this growing technology.

Don't ever feel like you are limited in what you can accomplish with crypto-currency because like the internet in 1994, no one yet knows where it is going or how it will completely change our lives.

Now head over to Coinbase and let's get started together on this journey to wealth in crypto. Invest as much or as little as you can afford – the amount does not matter right now. You can invest $1 if you want, but it's better to start now rather than waste any more time. Get your own financial breakthrough started today!

Chapter 13: Good Luck!

Thank you for reading this book about crypto-currency and congratulations on taking the first step to becoming an investor in crypto. In this book I have attempted to describe at what crypto-currency is, what some of its advantages and disadvantages are, it's use cases, how to securely hold your coins, how to mine them, where you can go to get an account setup to buy, sell or trade in crypto, what some of the biggest coins are as well as their outlook and lastly what trading strategy I would recommend for crypto investments. With that said, there are a lot of details and areas that I have purposefully not discussed in this publication due to the intended audience. Some readers may feel that I'm doing a disservice to competing coins or not giving enough credit where it's due to the coins mentioned.

For this, I'd like to welcome your comments and will gladly edit and release an updated 3rd edition in the future, hopefully after we've all made money on crypto coins.

For the people just joining me here, thank you for reading and supporting my writing. I greatly appreciate your support. When I published the first edition, all I had was an idea of writing a short eBook about a hobby and passion of mine.

That resulted in plenty of sales and a lot of great feedback for this edition.

I took that feedback and added in new sections, went back through the older sections, expanded on my ideas and thoughts from before, updated price targets and figures and generally tried to put together the best book I could for the time period.

I've read my competitor's books, attended a master class or three on crypto-currency, read my share of articles and followed a lot on twitter to gain the insights required to further this book along. As I sit here typing, I can honestly say that this book is as good as anyone else's book for people looking to get started except it also contains step by step directions for areas that have previously been left to the reader to figure out on their own.

If you've enjoyed this book, you would be helping me out tremendously if you left a positive review on Amazon. It supports my writing in the future the more good reviews I receive. If you have found this book to be lacking in areas or wish to critique it, please send me an email at **CryptoBrooks@gmail.com** I welcome any and all feedback as it only makes my writing better.

I would also like to thank my family and friends for listening to me talk about crypto-currency, updates on my writing and so much more for the last year or so. Without your selective listening, we'd all be tired of the subject.

The author would like to thank his wife Sara, his dog Mario, Schmoe the cat, Reddit, Google, Twitter, CNN, NY Times, Bloomberg and any other site that has run headlines in the mainstream news about alt coins and crypto-currency.

If you would like to donate Bitcoin to help me prepare for another book, you can send it to my address listed on the next page or scan the code.

1C4gZQivPfujSzdqqYcT7hKnz8LEUFXSpC

Any and all donations are greatly appreciated.

To those venturing out into investing in crypto after reading this, Good Luck! You will make some money if you practice patience!

 Thank you!

- D.M.Brooks

Works Cited

Chapter 1:

Zimbabwe 100 Trillion Dollars photo
http://www.CNN.com. Accessed 25 July 2017.

Bitcoin price over time photo
https://99bitcoins.com/price-chart-history/
Accessed 27 September 2017.

Chapter 2:

Blockchain
https://en.wikipedia.org/wiki/Blockchain.
Accessed 25 July 2017.

JP Morgan's Dimon says "Bitcoin is a Fraud"
https://www.reuters.com/article/legal-us-usa-banks-conference-jpmorgan/jpmorgans-dimon-says-bitcoin-is-a-fraud-idUSKCN1BN2PN Accessed 28 September 2017.

Chapter 3:

Technological Growth Curve chart from:
Crossing the Chasm, Geoffrey A. Moore 3rd Edition 2014
Google Images for the chart, accessed 23 September, 2017

Chapter 4:

IRS rules from IRS.Gov
https://www.irs.gov/newsroom/irs-virtual-currency-guidance

Additional tax information courtesy of Turbo Tax

https://turbotax.intuit.com/tax-tools/tax-tips/Taxes-101/Tax-Tips-for-Bitcoin-and-Virtual-Currency/INF29402.html

Chapter 5:

Bitcoin prices over time chart. Money Minded.
https://www.facebook.com/permalink.php?id=1951736161706253&story_fbid=1953020834911119 Accessed 26 July 2017.

Segwit description
http://www.investopedia.com/terms/s/segwit-segregated-witness.asp Accessed 24 September 2017.

Lightning Network Advantages Description

http://lightning.network/how-it-works/
Accessed 24 September 2017.

Chapter 8:

Bitcoin mining information from:

https://www.coinish.com Accessed 5 October
2017.

https://www.cryptocompare.com Accessed 5
October 2017.

https://www.bitcoinmining.com Accessed 5
October 2017.

Chapter 9:

Candlestick Pattern chart from Google
Images. Accessed 1 October 2017.

Chapter 10:

Coin market cap for Bitcoin

https://coinmarketcap.com/ Accessed 29 September 2017

Chapter 11:

JP Morgan's Dimon says "Bitcoin is a Fraud"

https://www.reuters.com/article/legal-us-usa-banks-conference-jpmorgan/jpmorgans-dimon-says-bitcoin-is-a-fraud-idUSKCN1BN2PN Accessed 28 September 2017.

Bitcoin price over time photo

https://99bitcoins.com/price-chart-history/ Accessed 27 September 2017.

CNBC Bitcoin

https://www.cnbc.com/video/2017/09/14/tom-lee-heres-why-bitcoin-will-hit-25000.html

Chapter 12:

www.twitter.com

Candlestick chart:

http://www.comtradein.com/candle-stick-chart/